Cooking with Rice

PAUL EVE

FARRAR, STRAUS AND GIROUX
NEW YORK

Library of Congress Cataloging in Publication Data

Eve, Paul.
Cooking with rice.
1. Cookery (Rice)   I. Title.
TX809.R5E9   641.6'3'18   74–4321

ACKNOWLEDGMENTS

The author and publishers wish to express their grateful thanks to the following for their assistance in compiling this book: Mr. and Mrs. Rex Elliott, Mrs. Carole Fahy, Señor Manuel and Señora Carmen Garzaran, Miss Elaine Chubb, Mr. Ray Horricks, Lesley Scott of the Rice Council and Bette Lehne of the Rice Information Service (in England), Anton Wills-Eve, the Conimex Company of Holland, and the Department of Trade at Australia House.

CONTENTS

Introduction

The deeper you delve into the subject of rice, the more you realize its importance to the world. But when the mind has grasped the fact that every second human being on this globe gets four fifths of his nourishment from rice, it still boggles at the extent of its use, the amount of dependence placed on it by so many millions, and how versatile it can be.

Is it the world's greatest single food? What other, for instance, is so versatile as to figure equally in soups, appetizers, fish dishes and many entrées, main courses, desserts, cakes, and pastries? It may even provide the aperitif before the meal, the wine to be drunk with it, or the liqueur to follow, such as arrack. In the East, where it originated, it remains the staple food of rich and poor alike, and, more than that, it is the central element of many people's lives. Many legends and superstitions have evolved around it in the East, where men's lives depend on it.

Today the world food situation is developing in such a way that rice may become as important a food in the West as it is in the East. The population explosion, the arrival of the so-called affluent society, and various other factors are combining to push the price of foods which have been part of the staple Western diet for years to heights beyond many people's reach, and the indications are that, ironic as it may be, the more affluent we become, the less likely we will be able to afford the high prices that some foods will cost. Rice, on the other hand, is less likely to rise as much in price as many other foods, and it presents a very healthy and pleasant way of eking out expensive cuts of meat or other main foods. Properly handled, therefore, it could be an important factor in trying to keep down the rocketing cost of living without resorting to less healthy extra portions of bread, potatoes, and other cheap filler foods.

Personally I love, and always have loved, rice in most of its forms, and I have always been fascinated by the almost infinite number of images it can present to the cook. Unfortunately, to a great many people who suffered at an early age from a badly cooked rice masquerading as boiled rice or rice pudding, rice may present unpleasant memories. I hope that in the pages that follow some of these may be eradicated and replaced by the promise of a highly tasty pilaf or a magnificent risotto, or some of the national dishes with which rice goes as eggs go with bacon. However, it seemed pointless to include many recipes from the Far East that would have involved the use of ingredients not available in this country. Some, obviously, have crept into the book as an illustration of what is done in the countries concerned, and you may well find now that, with the great expansion of specialty and health food stores in this country in recent years, some ingredients are not as unavailable as you may have thought.

The amount of rice recommended for one person varies from country to country and you may vary the quantities according to the appetites or tastes of your family or guests; generally throughout the book they are based on two or three ounces per person of raw rice, which, when cooked, will be equal to six or nine ounces. But don't be afraid of cooking too much: it will keep in the refrigerator for a week or more and can easily be reheated in a buttered dish in the oven, and you will find that in this and a dozen other ways it is a really obliging food.

We have not mentioned wild rice in the book because it is, strictly speaking, not a rice but a native American cereal whose high price and distinctive flavor make it best suited to a few special-occasion dishes.

P.E.

COOKING WITH RICE

The Story of Rice

The story of rice begins with the beginning of time itself, for no one has yet discovered at what stage in the development of man this incredible food came into existence. We know that it existed 5,000 years before Christ, so it is at least 7,000 years old, but rice could well be very much older than that. There is recorded evidence that 2,800 years before Christ a Chinese emperor ordered that the planting of the rice crop should be turned into a ceremonial occasion, and there are references to rice in the ancient scriptures of some other Far East countries. Some historians claim that it originated in the south of India and was exported from there to China, Japan, and Southeast Asia, but there is also considerable support for the theories which suggest that it originated in China. There is also evidence that irrigation fields for growing rice were in existence on the banks of the Yangtse River in China 2,500 years B.C. Were these copied from those on the banks of the great rivers of India, or was it from there that traders crossing into India took samples of the new food and the knowledge of how to grow it? In the long run the question will occupy only the academic mind in search of historic truth: for our purposes it is sufficient that rice developed in the East and moved westward with various civilizations.

The extent to which it is the staple food in so many Eastern countries and the importance it plays in the lives of millions of Asians tend to indicate that it has always been there. To most Asian peoples it is life itself. The custom of throwing rice at newly married couples, now practiced widely throughout the world, came originally from India and China, because rice is the symbol of fertility there. In parts of Indonesia no girl is thought to be fit for marriage unless she can cook a bowl of rice perfectly; rice, say the Indonesians, is the gift of the goddess Dewie Srie and therefore the bride must know how to handle it perfectly. In Japanese mythology the sun goddess sowed rice in the fields of heaven and gave some of the sprouts to the emperor's descendants to plant on earth.

It could have been a couple of thousand years before Christ when rice traveled westward into Persia and from there to other Middle Eastern areas. Certainly it is known to have been cultivated in Egypt 400 years B.C. Previously, Sophocles had referred to it in his writings and Alexander the Great is said to have carried it on his campaigns more than 300 years B.C. When the Moors occupied parts of Spain centuries later they took rice with them from North Africa and established it as a food in Spain. How firmly it took root is witnessed by the amount grown and eaten there today and by the number of Spanish dishes based on rice. Some historians say it was introduced into Italy by Marco Polo in the thirteenth century, but it is far more likely to have reached the West, and Italy, over the Silk Road long before Marco Polo's famous journeys were undertaken.

Nonetheless, it was not firmly established in Italy until the sixteenth century. Early efforts to grow it and make it a popular food in France about the same time were doomed to failure. The French, in fact, appear to have disliked rice: during the famine caused by the Siege of Paris in 1870 and 1871, when there was no bread and Parisians were reduced to eating cats, dogs, rats, and the like, large stocks of rice remained untouched. But since then the French have become more rice-minded, and it is grown successfully in the Camargue region of Southern France.

It was quite by accident, apparently, that rice got to the New World in 1694. The captain of a sailing vessel on the way from Madagascar had to put into the port of Charleston, in what is now South Carolina, for repairs, and he gave the colonists some of the rice he had on board. They started growing it and four years later exported the first consignment of sixty tons to England. The name Carolina rice stuck—the French still call it *riz Caroline*—although it is many years now since it was found to grow better in Louisiana, Texas, Arkansas, California, and Mississippi. The industry that sent its sixty tons to Britain at the end of the seventeenth century now exports at the rate of more than 300 million dollars' worth a year—indeed, it is from the United States that Britain gets most of her rice.

Attempts were made to grow rice in Australia in the early days of colonization but were unsuccessful. It was not until after World War I that a strain of rice from California was found to be suitable and could be grown in some parts of Australia, such as the Murrumbidgee Irrigation Area of New South Wales and in the valley of the Murray River. In World War II the need for new sources of rice to fill the gaps caused by the Japanese occupation of parts of Southeast Asia gave a great fillip to the Australian industry, and production, now highly mechanized, has moved toward the quarter-million-tons-a-year mark. Australia is the second biggest supplier of rice to Britain.

Total world production of rice is somewhere in the region of 250 million tons per year, and about nine tenths of this is in China, Japan, Indonesia, the Philippines, and other Asian countries. China alone produces more than one third of the world total.

What is rice?

Rice is a cereal that grows on a grass-like stalk between two and four feet tall. It needs a temperate climate and thrives best in tropical or subtropical climates so that it can ripen in a temperature of about 85° F., though it does also grow in other areas.

It needs a lot of water—300 gallons to grow one pound, according to the scientists. The ideal rice field, therefore, is one that can be flooded to a depth of at least a few inches and may also be drained off later. In the old days—and still in primitive areas—the fields were hand-plowed before the monsoons and the rice planted just after the first of the monsoon rain had fallen. As heavy rain flooded the land, the shoots would rise above the water and the ripe rice would be harvested after the floodwaters had dried. In modern rice-growing areas the whole business is mechanized: seeds are sown from airplanes, the floodwaters are mechanically controlled, and the rice itself harvested by modern mechanical monsters.

When the rice is first harvested and is in its rough state it is called paddy. (If some of the stalks are left, as in some Eastern countries, it is called stalk paddy.) When the inedible husk of the rice is removed, the edible inner part remains and is known as brown rice. This is highly nutritious, but most people prefer their rice milled, a process that removes the brown layers of bran on the outside and leaves a whitish or grayish grain of rice as we are used to seeing it. Nowadays the whole operation of husking and milling, as well as the initial cleaning of the paddy, is carried out in giant plants in which the rice enters as paddy at one end and emerges cleaned, milled, and probably packaged as well at the other end, although much transport of rice is done in bulk carriers, which are filled and emptied by suction pumps.

About two thirds of the weight of the paddy rice finishes up as table rice. From the rest are made such products as rice flour, ground rice, flaked rice, and so on. Rice flour and ground rice often figure in dishes for freezing because they have certain qualities that are also used in confectionery and some cosmetics. Not much of the rice is wasted: some of the bran milled from the outside of the grain is used in livestock feed, pet foods, or oil for human consumption, while the husk is used in industrial processes, for making packing materials, or even as a fuel.

Types of rice

There are, or so we are told, as many as 7,000 different types of rice, and since some industrious soul has obviously counted them, I am quite prepared to accept the word of the experts on the matter. But you are unlikely to hear of more than a mere handful, some of which will be obtainable only from specialty shops, since your local supermarket is hardly likely to carry more on its shelves than will be sold easily. So few people will know whether the rice they are cooking comes from Burma, or Thailand, or Louisiana, Italy or New South Wales. A real rice connoisseur (surely there cannot be many of such a race) could, in theory, pick up a few grains and, by looking at them, biting them, and smelling them, tell what part of what country they come from.

What you will find in the shops are long-grain, medium- and round- (or short-) grain rice, a type of treated rice known as parboiled, and some precooked or "instant rice." These are their main characteristics:

Extra-long-grain rice: The original long-grain rice came from Patna, in India, and the name has stuck to the same type of rice no matter where it is grown. (In some countries this is still the name it is sold under.) It is probably a long time since rice originating in Patna got on to the British market, but the type is successfully grown elsewhere. When milled, the grain is between four and five times as long as it is wide and translucent in appearance. If properly cooked, the grains should be fluffy and separate, making it ideal for plain boiled rice, or for curry, pilafs, and savory dishes. Basmati rice is similar but shorter and thinner.

Long-grain rice: This was the original Carolina rice, with a grain three times as long as it is thick. It is not as fine as the better-quality extra-long-grain and is used for croquettes, risottos, and the like, as well as for boiled rice.

Round-grain (or short-grain) rice: This is also called Chinese, Japanese, Java, etc., or sometimes pudding rice. It is much more sticky when cooked and so is excellent for puddings rather than savory dishes in which the grains should be separate. It is easier to grow, gives a bigger yield, and is therefore generally cheaper.

Italian rice: This is a round-grain type grown in Italy and, because of its ability to absorb more water than most other types, ideal for making the Italian risottos.

Parboiled ("Converted") rice: This is a type of easy-cook rice that has been subjected to a form of pressure cooking before it is milled. In the old days it was found that too much milling and polishing of rice increased the risk of beri-beri, since too much of the natural mineral and vitamin was removed. The parboiling process forces some of these health-giving elements from the outer brans into the heart of the grain itself, so that after milling it still retains much of its original goodness. The end result is a grain that separates better, although it takes a little longer to cook.

Precooked (*or instant*) *rice:* This rice (also known as "Minute" rice) has actually been cooked and then dried. It needs only to have the water restored, either by brief cooking or by soaking in boiling water.

Brown rice: Only the husk has been removed from this, leaving the nutty-tasting shells of bran with all their highly nutritious content still around the rice grain. Highly recommended as a health food.

Rice flour: This rice has gone through a milling process and is almost as fine as ordinary flour. It is used in baking and can be found in specialty stores and health food departments.

Ground rice: This is the coarsest form of milled rice; it has the consistency of granulated sugar. Although it sounds exotic, it can be found in any supermarket as the breakfast cereal Cream of Rice. It is used in making cakes and cookies.

How to cook it—the great controversy

Just about everyone who ever does any cooking will tell you that he or she knows *the* infallible way of cooking rice, and so it is not surprising that controversy has raged for many years over the various ways of doing it: to wash it first (in cold water) or afterward (in hot water), or not to wash it at all; to fry it first in oil, or not to fry it, and so on. If there are 7,000 different types of rice and rice is 7,000 years old at least, then there are probably 7,000 different ways of cooking it. Different customs have become established in different countries.

In China, one method is to wash it, then cook it by bringing it to a boil and simmering it in twice its volume of water in a tightly covered pan for 20 minutes, until the water is absorbed. There are many other Chinese methods of cooking rice.

In Japan they wash the rice in a number of changes of water, then soak it for several hours. Then they cook it with 1½ times its volume of water by bringing it to a boil, covering, boiling gently for 10 minutes, then simmering for 10 minutes and leaving it off the heat 10 minutes, all without opening the lid of the pan.

Indonesians do theirs like the Chinese, but wash it more thoroughly.

In Singapore they wash the rice three times, then throw it into fast-boiling water, at least three or four times its own volume, then boil it for 12 minutes, drain, and put it in a cool oven or on a very low heat on top of the range to dry out.

In India the rice is washed a number of times, put into plenty of fast-boiling water and cooked 20 minutes, then drained and rinsed with cold water.

In the Middle East, the Arabs wash the rice, dry it, put it into twice its volume of salted water, bring it to a boil, and cook it until the water is absorbed, then spread some butter over it and put it in the oven with the lid on the pan until it is almost dry.

Italians don't believe in washing it: they pick it over, then cook it in plenty of boiling stock (*not* water) for 20 minutes and test it by biting a grain in the same way as they do with spaghetti to see if it is *al dente*. If so, they put it into a buttered dish to dry out in a cool oven.

In America we put it into a large saucepan with twice its volume of water and some salt to taste, bring it to a boil, stir once, put a tight-fitting lid on the pan, and cook for 15 minutes, then test to see if it is cooked and if necessary cook it a few minutes more or until the liquid is absorbed. Then we turn it out of the pan in which it was cooked, fluff it up with a fork, and serve it hot.

The best way of cooking rice

The best way, of course, is the one you arrive at after experimenting with various types of rice cooking, but you will find that different methods suit different dishes. In some of the recipes given here, for example, it will be seen that rice is part-cooked by frying in oil with some of the ingredients and then cooked in stock, probably in the oven.

For plain boiled rice, however, I prefer the American method. Boiled rice can be flavored quite simply in these ways:

Chicken flavor: use chicken stock instead of water, or make up your own stock with a chicken cube and water.

Beef flavor: use beef stock (or a beef cube or spoonful of beef essence in the water) instead of plain water.

Tomato flavor: substitute canned tomato juice for half the water; a dash of sauce will add a little more taste.

Orange flavor: roast duck goes well with rice that has been cooked in orange juice, either fresh or canned, instead of water.

Lemon flavor: add several slices of lemon to the water when cooking.

Herbed rice: fresh chopped herbs and a little butter give a very delicate taste to rice; choose the herbs according to the dish.

All sorts of soup flavors may be obtained by using a few spoonfuls of soup instead of the equivalent amount of water when boiling the rice.

A few don'ts

Don't bother washing rice that comes in packets, particularly well-known brands. It has been well cleaned in the packaging process and certainly will not be improved by washing out some of the goodness before you cook it.

Restrain yourself while the rice is cooking. Opening the lid of the pot lets the steam out, reduces the temperature, and results in the rice being imperfectly cooked. Stirring has the same effect, and breaks up the rice grains, so don't do that either.

NATIONAL DISHES

Rice with the Chinese

Since it is probable that rice was cooked in China before it was cooked anywhere else, the Chinese might reasonably be supposed to know more about it than anyone else. In a country of hundreds of millions of people and at least a dozen different regional forms of cookery, it is not surprising that there is a very wide range of dishes that either contain rice or are meant to accompany it.

There are also many types of rice in China, so it is difficult to lay down any sort of general rule for Chinese rice cookery. However, if there is one rice dish that is typically Chinese and was invented by them, it is fried rice. This perhaps stems from the fact that they are thrifty people: to waste rice is regarded as wicked and certain to bring bad luck. The dish known in its thousands of forms as fried rice was therefore invented for using up excess rice. The Chinese also originated the various forms of flavored rice.

Rice is undoubtedly the basis of all Chinese food in many parts of the country, whether it be plain boiled or graced with exotic names such as only the Chinese can conjure up. Here are some of the ways they have of preparing rice and the dishes that go with it.

CHINESE BOILED RICE: 1

¼ cup rice per person
5 ounces water per person

Put the water in a saucepan, add the rice, and bring to a boil over high heat; keep at boiling for 5 or 6 minutes, then simmer for another 20 minutes with the lid on the pan, having stirred the rice once before putting the lid on. This rice should now be tender without being soft, and separate and virtually dry.

CHINESE BOILED RICE: 2

¼ cup rice per person
twice as much water as rice
salt

Measure the amount of rice you are cooking in cups and use double the number of cups of water in cooking it. First wash the rice under running water, until the water runs clear. Drain. Put rice into the measured amount of water as it reaches a boil, salt to taste, and bring to a boil again, stir, cover, and simmer for 20 minutes or until rice is tender. Remove lid and leave on heat for 2 minutes to complete drying out of rice before serving.

CHINESE STEAMED RICE

Measurements as for Chinese Boiled Rice 2, but blanch rice several minutes in boiling water, then place in top of a steamer with measured amount of water below and steam until dry, which should take about 1 hour.

CHINESE FRIED RICE

This is the recipe for the basic fried rice of China, which may be converted into an almost infinite number of savory dishes by the addition of various other ingredients.

3 ounces ham, finely chopped
vegetable oil (peanut oil if
   possible)
3 eggs
1¼ cups rice, cooked and cooled

4 scallions, finely chopped
monosodium glutamate
   (optional)
soy sauce

Fry the chopped ham in the minimum possible amount of oil. Remove from pan, add 2 tablespoons oil, heat; beat eggs well and put these and the cold rice into the pan together, stirring continuously. Add ham, scallions, monosodium glutamate, and about a tablespoon of soy sauce to the pan, cook and stir for 1 or 2 minutes at most, and serve.   *Serves 4.*

FRIED RICE WITH SHRIMP AND BAMBOO SHOOTS

1¼ cups rice
3 eggs
soy sauce
vegetable oil (peanut oil if possible)
¾ cup fresh peas
2 mushrooms, diced
4 slices bamboo shoot, chopped

4 ounces chicken or pork, cooked and chopped
4 ounces shelled large shrimp, chopped
4 scallions, chopped
monosodium glutamate (optional)

Boil the rice and let it cool. Beat the eggs and mix in about ½ tablespoon soy sauce. Put a little oil in pan and gently fry peas, mushrooms, and bamboo shoot, add meat, shrimp, and scallions, and season. Fry briefly at high temperature. In another pan heat 2 tablespoons oil, fry rice briefly in this, add contents of first pan, stir until reheated, then add egg mixture and stir rapidly until cooked.   *Serves 4.*

FRIED RICE WITH SHRIMP AND
CHINESE CABBAGE

vegetable oil (peanut oil if
   possible)
½ 8-ounce can water
   chestnuts, sliced
2 leaves Chinese cabbage,
   finely chopped
2 mushrooms, chopped
4 scallions, chopped
1¼ cups rice, cooked

3 ounces chicken, cooked
3 ounces ham, diced
soy sauce
monosodium glutamate
   (optional)
4 ounces shelled large shrimp,
   cooked
3 eggs, beaten and fried into a
   very thin omelette

Heat 2 tablespoons oil in a deep frying pan and add vegetables;
fry quickly over high heat. Add rice, chicken, and ham, soy sauce
and seasoning; stir until well mixed, then add shrimp. Chop the
omelette into very thin strips or very small pieces and mix in
with the other ingredients in the pan; serve very hot.   *Serves 4.*

CANTON RICE

1¼ cups rice
2½ cups chicken stock
1 tablespoon butter
1 egg, beaten and cooked as
   very thin omelette

2 ounces cooked ham,
   chopped finely

Wash the rice under running water until the water is clear. Heat
the stock in a saucepan and add the rice, bring to a boil, and
then reduce heat and simmer for 20 minutes. Drain rice and add
butter. Chop omelette into small pieces and add it and the
chopped ham to the rice, mix well over low heat, and serve.
Serves 4.

Other Fried Rice Dishes

Many other fried rice dishes can be concocted by an enterprising cook by using such additions to the ingredients as bean shoots, canned or frozen lobster, canned crab, chopped scallops, tomatoes, various vegetables, fruits such as pineapple, and so on. The list is as long as your imagination.

CHICKEN CHOP SUEY AND RICE

1 to 1¼ cups rice
4 dried mushrooms (or small fresh ones)
vegetable oil (peanut oil if possible)
¾ pound cooked chicken, diced
¾ pound bean sprouts (or equivalent canned)
¼ cup bamboo shoots, cut into thin strips

1 red pepper, chopped
1 medium-sized onion, chopped
1 teaspoon soy sauce
½ teaspoon sugar
salt and pepper
cornstarch
1 tablespoon dry sherry
1¼ cups chicken stock

Boil the rice in the Chinese fashion (pages 13–14), drain, and keep warm. If Chinese dried mushrooms are available, they should be soaked for about 20 minutes in warm water; whether dried or fresh, slice thinly. Heat about 2 tablespoons oil in a fairly deep pan, fry chicken and all vegetables in it over high heat, for about 4 minutes, stirring continually. Remove from heat and add soy sauce and sugar, and seasoning to taste. Stir the cornstarch (a good teaspoon should be enough) into the sherry, add to the mixture, pour the stock over, and bring to a boil. Keep stirring until the mixture thickens, then cook for 2 minutes more. Serve the rice separately. *Serves 4.*

SWEET AND SOUR CRISPY PORK WITH RICE

1¼ *cups rice*
1 *pound lean pork*

Batter:
1 *cup flour*
½ *teaspoon baking powder*
salt
1 *egg*

Sweet and sour sauce:
2 *tablespoons soy sauce*
1 *tablespoon cooking sherry*
1 *tablespoon vinegar*
1 *tablespoon brown sugar*
a few anise seeds
salt and pepper
cornstarch

fat or oil for deep frying

Cook the rice as for Chinese Boiled Rice. Cut the pork into bite-sized pieces, or 1-inch cubes. Simmer the pork gently (after bringing it to a boil) in enough water to cover, plus the soy sauce, sherry, vinegar, sugar, anise seeds, and salt and pepper to taste. After about 45 minutes it should be tender. Drain, but keep the liquid.

Make a batter of the flour, sifted with the baking powder and a pinch of salt, the egg lightly beaten, and about 5 ounces of water. This should be well beaten and will be improved by allowing it to stand for 15 minutes or more. Drop all the pieces of cooked pork into this and allow them to become well coated, stirring to help this process along. Take each piece of pork out with a toothpick or larding needle, drop into very hot fat, and deep-fry until the batter is a lovely golden color and quite crisp. Dry on absorbent kitchen paper and keep warm.

Add about a tablespoon of cornstarch, stirred in a little water, to the liquid in which the pork was boiled and boil up until it thickens. More stock may be needed if the sauce is too thick. Pour it over the crispy pork pieces and serve with the rice on the side. *Serves 4.*

CHICKEN CHOP SUEY WITH ALMONDS AND RICE

¾ *cup rice*
7 *ounces almonds, blanched*
vegetable oil
1 *onion, sliced*
4 *ounces bean sprouts*
  (*preferably fresh ones*)
2 *ounces mushrooms* (*dried*
  Chinese if possible)
¼ *cup bamboo shoots, sliced*

1 *carrot, sliced*
1 *green pepper, sliced*
1 *pound chicken meat,*
  uncooked
salt and pepper
2 *teaspoons cornstarch*
1 *tablespoon dry sherry*
1 *tablespoon soy sauce*
2 *teaspoons sugar*

Boil the rice, drain, and keep warm. Brown the almonds in a little oil, remove, and set aside. Now put the onions in the pan until they are soft but not browned, then the remaining vegetables; add the chicken, cut into large dice, and fry until it begins to color, stirring frequently and adding a little more oil as it colors. Then cook 5 minutes more. Season to taste. Mix together the cornstarch, sherry, soy sauce, and sugar with not more than 1¼ cups water and stir into the pan. Add the almonds, increase heat, and stir until the pan mixture is thickened. Serve on a bed of the previously boiled rice or with rice on the side.   *Serves 4.*

PORK CHOP SUEY AND RICE

1 *cup rice*
2 *ounces mushrooms* (*if*
  possible Chinese dried
  mushrooms)
vegetable oil
2 *onions, sliced*
1 *pound lean pork, cut into*
  small cubes

8 *ounces bean sprouts*
¼ *cup bamboo shoots, sliced*
2 *teaspoons cornstarch*
1 *tablespoon dry sherry*
1 *tablespoon soy sauce*
2 *teaspoons sugar*

Boil the rice, drain, and set aside; keep warm. If the mushrooms are the dried type, soak them for 15 minutes in warm water, then slice. If not, just slice them. Heat a little oil and fry the onions until they begin to brown, then add the meat and cook for a few minutes, then add the bean sprouts, bamboo shoots, and the liquid obtained by blending the cornstarch, sherry, soy sauce, and sugar with about 1¼ cups water. Increase the heat and cook for 5 minutes, then reduce it and simmer for 5 minutes more. The sauce should be thick. Serve with the rice.   *Serves 4.*

SWEET AND SOUR FISH WITH RICE

1 cup rice	4 tablespoons vinegar
1 pound sole fillets	4 tablespoons sugar
1 carrot	2 heaping teaspoons cornstarch
1 green pepper	1 tablespoon soy sauce
1 onion	1 teaspoon finely chopped
1 heaping tablespoon mixed	fresh ginger
pickles, drained	1 tomato, peeled and chopped
3 stalks celery	1 teaspoon grated lemon peel
vegetable oil	salt

Boil the rice, drain and keep warm. Cut the fish into 1-inch squares. Slice the carrot and green pepper julienne fashion; chop the onion and the mixed pickles. Cut the celery stalks in halves lengthwise, then into 1-inch lengths. Fry the fish until cooked in a little oil, remove, and drain. Blend the vinegar, sugar, cornstarch, and soy sauce with a couple of tablespoons of water; pour any excess oil from the pan, add the blended liquid, cook over high heat for a few minutes; then reduce heat and add remaining ingredients; cook for 3 minutes more. Add fish, and when the fish is heated through, serve with bowl of rice on the side.   *Serves 4.*

BEEF AND ONIONS WITH RICE

One of the classic dishes on a Chinese table; in the West it is sufficient to stand by itself with rice instead of being one of many dishes. The onions can be replaced by various other vegetables if desired.

1 *pound good-quality frying steak*	1 *tablespoon cornstarch*
2 *teaspoons finely chopped fresh ginger*	2 *tablespoons soy sauce*
	salt
	¾ cup rice
2 *tablespoons dry sherry*	*vegetable oil*
2 *tablespoons sugar*	2 *large onions, sliced*

Lay the meat on a chopping board, and with a very sharp knife slice it lengthwise into pieces about ¼ inch thick. Lay each slice flat and cut it again so that the whole steak finishes up in strips the length of the original steak and about ¼ inch by ¼ inch. Make a marinade of all the other ingredients except the onion, oil, and rice, and soak the beef in this marinade for an hour. During that time boil the rice, drain, and keep warm.

Heat a couple of spoons of oil in a pan and fry the onions until tender but not browned. Remove the onions and keep warm, then add a little more oil, drain the beef, and fry it in the oil for about 1½ minutes, then add onion, mixing it well with the beef, and cook for 1 minute more. Serve with a bed of rice. *Serves 4.*

EIGHT PRECIOUS DUCK

The Chinese have a delightful habit of naming some of their dishes in a quaint way. Ten Precious Rice, for instance, is rice with 10 different ingredients to flavor it. Eight Treasures Rice is a well-known dish that we would regard as a dessert. Eight Precious Duck is duck with a stuffing of eight different items.

1 duck
2½ cups chicken stock
  (optional)

Stuffing:
½ cup medium-grain rice
4 ounces ham, diced

2 ounces small shelled shrimp
½ 8-ounce can water chestnuts
½ 10-ounce package frozen peas
4 ounces garlic sausage, diced
¼ cup pitted dates
½ cup mushrooms, chopped
salt to taste

Mix the stuffing ingredients well and place inside the bird. Sew up the cavity. The duck may now be steamed in the top of a steamer saucepan until cooked, for about 2 hours or more if needed, or it may be put into a casserole with the chicken stock and cooked in a moderate oven (350° F.) for 1 hour, then for another hour at 325° F.

Although there is rice in the stuffing, more rice may be served with the duck if desired.   *Serves 6.*

Chinese Leftovers

The Chinese make no bones about using yesterday's cold rice, and some other foods too, in today's food. This is mainly because rice lends itself so well to being reheated, and some dishes, like those based on beef and chicken, improve on being dished up again.

What you choose obviously will depend on what you have on hand. Cold rice will reheat easily in a little water, or in the pan with a piece of butter. When reheating the meat dishes, add a little soy sauce and sherry. These dishes are usually served on top of the rice rather than with the rice separate.

Rice with the Japanese

I often wonder what the hundred-million-odd Japanese would have done if rice had never been invented or, since it was not originally indigenous to Japan, if it had never crossed the sea from the mainland to Japan. Not only is it part of breakfast, lunch, and dinner—and snacks in between—but it is also part of Japanese tradition, superstition, and religion. It is as important to Japanese of all classes as bread is to the Western world. More than half the cultivated area of Japan, and that certainly includes every square inch that can be cultivated, is devoted to rice growing, and even this barely produces enough. Whatever other delicately prepared and elegantly displayed food dishes may be on a Japanese table, rice is always there too, sometimes plain-boiled, sometimes prepared in other ways, to do the real work of appeasing hunger. To eat every last grain of Japanese rice offered by your host is to honor him, but to leave any is grossly discourteous: in Japanese legends all sorts of dire fates await those foolhardy enough to waste any of the precious grains, as parents are keen to impress on children unwilling to finish off their rice bowl. Rice comes hot with hot fish, cold with cold or raw fish, often just plain-boiled, and sometimes at the end of a meal. It is not unusual to see small balls of cooked rice being eaten during a theater performance or a sporting event or, for that matter, just about anywhere at any time of day or night.

Rice in the Sushiya

Not only do the Japanese eat their rice at breakfast, lunch, and dinner, but it pops up in between in the numerous *sushi* bars dotted over the land. To call a *sushiya* or *sushi* bar a snack bar would hardly be doing it justice: more likely a bistro or a bar would be right, except that instead of going to a *sushiya* to drink, the Japanese go there to relax and eat a wide range of snacks that have different toppings on a bed of vinegared rice. What they drink—beer or green tea—is incidental to the rice snacks, which are made up to the customer's order. The *sushi* maker is a master at the art of scooping out just the right amount—almost to the very last grain—of cooked rice needed to make an oval raft about 2 inches long and an inch wide, pressing it in his palm so that it sticks together, and then topping it with whatever the customer selects. *Sushi* are usually served in pairs; or the customer may prefer some of the pressed *sushi* that can be bought in boxes.

Quite obviously it would not be possible in the Western world to recapture the authentic atmosphere of such Japanese establishments, but the *sushi* dishes can be adapted to our ways, particularly as an appetizer or part of an hors d'oeuvre. The rice should be starchy (polished rice in this case is preferable) and should be cooked only sufficiently to make it tender—about 15 minutes of simmering after being brought to the boil. The amount of water used will be the equivalent number of ounces to ounces of raw rice, plus 2 ounces of water. Remove from the heat and leave for 10 minutes before uncovering the pot.

For 2 cups of rice, make a vinegar sauce of 2 tablespoons of cider vinegar, a pinch of monosodium glutamate (optional), a teaspoon of salt, and 1½ tablespoons of sugar, by boiling all the ingredients in a saucepan for a few minutes and then removing the pan from the heat. The rice, which should have been kept hot, is placed in a bowl and the hot sauce poured over it and quickly mixed in. A fan (I use a little battery-operated electric one) will help to cool the rice quickly and produce a shiny surface on it.

This *sushi* rice may now be fashioned into small patties or rafts of whatever shape you fancy and topped with a wide range of foods. I doubt whether your guests would be very enthusiastic about some traditional toppings such as raw fish, including raw octopus, but they will certainly like those topped with shrimp, crab, hard-boiled egg or strips of omelette, mussels, bits of salad vegetable—the limit to choice being the limit of your ingenuity.

Pressed Sushi (*Oshizushi*)

Some of the toppings mentioned above can also be used for another form of *sushi*, ideal for cocktail parties, Sunday morning drinks, or a light hors d'oeuvre for a meal. The basis is rice as prepared for an ordinary *sushi*. Make enough to half-fill a cake tin with a removable bottom, square, oblong, round, or whatever shape comes to hand. Simmer some sliced mushrooms and carrots for a few minutes in a couple of tablespoons of soy sauce, the same quantity of *mirin* (sweet rice wine) or sherry, a pinch of monosodium glutamate, if desired, some thin slices of cucumber, a tablespoon of sugar, and a couple of tablespoons of water. Drain the liquid off and set the vegetables aside. Now make a thin omelette with 2 eggs, and cut it into 1-inch squares. Shell some large shrimp, slice them in halves lengthwise, then cut them into smaller pieces. Cut some sliced smoked salmon into squares slightly smaller than the squares of omelette.

Keeping a bowl of water handy to moisten your fingers, pack some *sushi* rice into whatever dish you have and press it down hard. Spread a layer of vegetables over this, then another layer of *sushi* rice, and press down again. Mix a little horseradish sauce with enough water to thin it down a little and spread over the top of the rice. Now place squares of omelette, each topped by a square of smoked salmon and a piece of shrimp, over the whole surface, cover with some greaseproof paper, and press down with either a piece of wood of the right shape or another dish. Put a heavy weight on top and leave for half an hour. Remove weights and paper and cut the *oshizushi* into squares around the squares of omelette and serve, with a little sauce or pickle if desired. There is almost no limit to the number of variations on this dish, the main requirement being that the *sushi* rice is of the right consistency to take the other foods.

JAPANESE CHICKEN AND VEGETABLE RICE

1½ cups rice	3 tablespoons mirin (sweet
½ medium-sized chicken, boned	rice wine—or sherry
1 large carrot	will do)
4 ounces button mushrooms	soy sauce

Wash the rice in running water until the water is quite clear, then drain for 1 hour. While it is draining, cut the chicken into small strips and the carrot and mushrooms into thin slices or strips. Put the chicken, mushrooms, carrot, wine, and about 2 tablespoons soy sauce into a pot and bring to a boil, then remove from heat. Let this stand for ½ hour, then add the rice and 1 pint water, cover with tight-fitting lid, bring to a boil, then reduce heat and simmer gently for 18 minutes. Remove from heat and allow the pot to rest for another 10 minutes before removing the lid and serving.   *Serves 4.*

RICE WITH TEMPURA

One of the great joys of Japanese cuisine is *tempura,* the Japanese equivalent of batter-cooked fish, shellfish, vegetables, and so on. The main difference is that the Japanese version is coated in a batter that far surpasses most of those used in the West. It may be served with or without rice, but *tempura* pieces placed over a large bowl of rice (or individual small ones) and covered with a tempura sauce works well.

TEMPURA

Collect enough shrimp (halve them if very large), bits of lobster and crab, sliced fillets of sole or other white fish, and bits of herring, scallops, other fish, and also some sliced carrots, broken green beans, pieces of sweet potato, pumpkin, etc., for 4 persons. These should be deep-fried very briefly after being dipped in flour and *tempura* batter.

TEMPURA BATTER

1 egg
1¼ cups chilled water
¾ cup flour

⅛ teaspoon baking soda
¼ cup cornstarch

Beat up the egg and add the water, which should have been chilled well in the refrigerator; mix the water and egg until light, then sift into the liquid the flour, baking soda, and cornstarch; keeping the bowl over ice if possible. Mix for only a few seconds: overmixing will spoil the dish, and it does not matter if there are lumps in the batter. The thinner the batter, incidentally, the more delicate will be the cooked result. There is nothing worse than a soggy *tempura*, produced by a batter that is too thick, although for the vegetables it may be a little heavier than for fish, etc. Some Eastern gourmets like a little sesame seed oil mixed with the oil used for cooking to impart just a little extra taste to the batter. *Makes enough to coat tempura for 4 persons.*

TEMPURA SAUCE

There are many recipes for a sauce to accompany the *tempura*. This is a popular one.

1¼ cups chicken stock
2 tablespoons dry sherry
2 tablespoons soy sauce
pinch monosodium glutamate
   (optional)

1 tablespoon sugar
1 teaspoon ground ginger
1 small white turnip, grated

Bring all the ingredients except turnip to a boil, simmer for a few minutes, and add grated turnip.

When the rice has been cooked, the sauce made, and the *tempura* rushed from the deep-fryer and placed on the rice, either in a large bowl or in small individual ones, the dish is covered with sauce and immediately eaten. It is then called *tendon,* a contraction of the two words *tempura* and *donburi* (originally the name for the bowl, but eventually for what was in it).

JAPANESE GINGER RICE

Rice often figures as a separate course in Japanese meals, either plain-boiled or in a flavored form, as in this recipe.

1½ cups rice	*2 tablespoons dry sherry*
2 tablespoons chopped fresh ginger	*2 tablespoons soy sauce*

Wash the rice under running water, then soak for an hour and drain; put the rice, ginger, sherry, and soy sauce into a heavy pan with 1 pint of water, bring to a boil, reduce heat, cover the pan tightly, and simmer for 20 minutes, or until the liquid is absorbed.   *Serves 4.*

CEREMONIAL RICE AND RED BEANS (*Sekihan*)

This is a dish used in Japan for ceremonial occasions, such as the birthday of the reigning emperor or similar celebrations.

For four people, it is made with 1½ cups of rice and the same weight of dried red *azuki* beans, which can be bought at specialty stores. The beans should be soaked overnight.

The rice should be washed under running water until absolutely all signs of anything but rice in the water have disappeared. Drain it in a colander or sieve for 1 hour or more before cooking. Put it into a saucepan with 2¼ cups of cold water, bring gently to a boil, reduce heat, and simmer for 20 minutes, or until rice is almost dry. Drain red beans, put them into water, and boil for 1 hour. Drain and mix with rice and cook in a steamer for 1 hour before serving.

Rice with the Indonesians

When it comes to the Indonesians and their rice dishes, you might almost call the whole thing Dutch. In three and a half centuries of colonial rule over these islands, the Dutch incorporated many forms of Indonesian food into their own cuisine. Though rice had, of course, been in use in Holland before the Dutch colonized the islands, it assumed a new dimension when some of the Indonesian foods and spices to go with them were imported into Holland. The Dutch people learned the joys of the *rijsttafel*, or rice table, that magnificent and colorful array of highly spiced foods and relishes ranged around the central piece, a great bowl of steaming boiled rice sitting on a warming plate or over a small spirit lamp to keep it warm. The meal has rice as its basis: the numerous side dishes might appear to Western eyes at first as mere appetizers, but in this context they form a whole meal—a meal as full, for example, as some of the Scandinavian smorgasbords, which also are made up of many small pieces.

In Holland the *rijsttafel* is very popular and all the necessary ingredients are readily available. In America most can be bought in delicatessens or specialty stores. You may be able to find, in specialty stores, some of the spices and relishes marketed, ready-mixed or ready to prepare, by the Dutch company Conimex.' Here, then, is how the Indonesians prepare rice, with a dozen or so side dishes to serve at a *rijsttafel*.

INDONESIAN BOILED RICE

1½ cups long-grain rice
salt
water

The Indonesians believe in washing the rice over and over again before starting to cook it. Roughly speaking, the more water the rice is cooked in, the softer it will be. Thus for a rice which is to be fairly hard, such as that to be fried afterward, less water should be used than for a rice that will be served as a bed for other foods. After washing the rice in cold water 4 or 5 times (until the water in which it is washed remains clear), the rice is drained and then put into water with some salt to taste and brought to a boil. If the rice is to be hard-cooked, the volume of water should be 1½ times that of the dry rice, or 2¼ cups. If it is to be soft-cooked, add 3 cups water. When it reaches the boiling point, reduce the heat and put the lid on the pan and cook for 20 minutes. Some Indonesians maintain the lid should not be lifted nor the rice stirred until it is cooked, but a more practical way is to look at the rice after, say, 15 minutes to make sure it has not dried out. You can tell when the rice is finally cooked by pressing a grain in your fingers.

Among the many side dishes that may be offered with a *rijsttafel* are a mixed vegetable soup (*sajoer tjampoer*), so thick that it is more like a salad, spiced fish (*boemboe ikan*), which may be broiled or baked, chicken, pork, or lamb *sateh* or pieces of meat broiled on skewers and covered with a sauce based on peanuts, hard-boiled eggs in a spiced sauce, a mixture of coconut and peanuts, large shrimp-flavored crisps called *kroepoek oedang,* and a variety of *sambals,* or relishes, and mango chutney. The chutney, shrimp crisps, and some of the relishes may be bought already prepared, the crisps being ready to deep-fry in hot oil or fat; if you want to make up some of the *sambals* for yourself, some of the spices may be purchased at your local delicatessen, others are available at specialty shops. The following side dishes will each serve about 4 people.

MIXED VEGETABLE SOUP (*Sajoer Tjampoer*)

4 ounces stewing beef
1⅓ cups shredded or flaked
   coconut
¼ cup butter
1 onion, sliced
1 clove garlic, crushed
½ teaspoon ground coriander
pinch of ground turmeric
½ teaspoon ground ginger
½ teaspoon trassie (*strong*
   shrimp paste)

2 teaspoons sambal oelek
   (*or chili powder*)
1 pound (*3 to 4 cups*)
   coarsely chopped white
   cabbage, cauliflower, carrots,
   green beans, and bean sprouts
   in equal quantities
1 bay leaf
salt and pepper

Cut the beef into small pieces and set it to simmer in 1¼ pints of water with a little salt. It may simmer for an hour if you wish, but 1 pint of stock is required from it. While it is cooking, soak the coconut in 1½ pints boiling water for 1 hour, stirring occasionally. Strain the coconut and squeeze it out into the liquid, then discard the coconut. The liquor is known as *santen,* or coconut milk.

Heat the butter in a heavy stockpot, lightly fry the onion and garlic, add coriander, turmeric, ginger, *trassie*, and *sambal oelek*, and cook 3 minutes, then add the vegetables and cook for 2 minutes more. Add the beef stock, *santen*, bay leaf, and seasoning if required and bring to a boil; cook until the vegetables are only barely cooked and serve in a tureen or vegetable bowl as part of the *rijsttafel*.

SPICED FISH   (*Boemboe Ikan*)

1½ *pounds firm white fish*
  fillets
½ *cup butter*
2 *onions, chopped*
1 *clove garlic, crushed*
3 *tablespoons lemon juice*
2 *teaspoons* sambal oelek (*or
  chili powder*)

½ *teaspoon* trassie (*shrimp
  paste*)
1½ *tablespoons soy sauce*
½ *teaspoon turmeric*
1 *tablespoon tomato ketchup*

Fry the fish fillets in butter, remove, and drain. Add onions and garlic to the pan and brown, then add remaining ingredients, except ketchup, and boil the sauce well, adding the tomato ketchup just before serving the sauce over the fish. The dish is part of the *rijsttafel*.

THE SATEHS

There are various *satehs* in Indonesian cookery, made of beef, pork, chicken, lamb, and so on, the meat cubed and threaded onto skewers in the manner of kebabs farther west; the word *sateh* means "grilled" or "broiled." The meat is generally marinated first and, after broiling, is served with a sauce usually based on peanut butter or on soy sauce.

Sateh Babi (pork), Sateh Ajam (chicken), and Sateh Kambing (lamb) are all cooked the same way. The following recipe for Sateh Babi may be adapted for other meats.

SATEH BABI

1½ pounds lean pork meat, cut into 1-inch cubes

Marinade:
2 cloves garlic, chopped
3 tablespoons vegetable oil
½ pint santen *(see page 31)*
1 tablespoon clear honey
3 tablespoons soy sauce
salt and pepper

Sauce:
liquid from marinade
1 teaspoon sambal oelek *(or chili powder)*
4 tablespoons peanut butter
1 tablespoon lemon juice

To make the marinade: fry the garlic in oil a few minutes; add *santen*, honey, soy sauce, salt, and pepper and bring to a boil; boil until thick. Cool. Marinate the meat cubes in this overnight, or at least for several hours. Thread the meat cubes onto metal (or, traditionally, Indonesian bamboo) skewers and cook under hot broiler, basting with a little oil if needed.

To make the sauce: add to the marinade liquid the ingredients for the sauce and boil up, adding a little water if needed. Pour the sauce over the broiled meat, on the skewers, and serve as a side dish for *rijsttafel*.

SHORT-CUT SATEH

Satehs can be cooked much more quickly (but suffer, obviously, from less flavor) by rubbing the cubes of meat with salt, pepper, and honey, leaving them for half an hour, and then broiling with some oil for basting.

A sort of general *sateh* sauce can be made with 4 tablespoons peanut butter, 1 teaspoon treacle or syrup, 1 tablespoon soy sauce, 1 teaspoon chili powder, 1 teaspoon lemon juice, and 1 clove of garlic, crushed. Place all the ingredients in a pan with a little water (according to how thick you like the sauce) and bring slowly to a boil, then simmer for 10 minutes more.

HARD-BOILED EGGS IN SPICED SAUCE

8 *hard-boiled eggs, shelled and quartered lengthwise*

Sauce:
1 *clove garlic, crushed*
½ *teaspoon ground ginger (or fresh ginger)*
2 *teaspoons* sambal oelek *(or chili powder)*

1 *onion, chopped*
½ *teaspoon* trassie
2 *tablespoons good-quality vegetable oil*
½ *pint* santen *(see page 31)*
1 *bay leaf*
1 *teaspoon brown sugar (or honey)*

Fry the garlic, ginger, *sambal oelek*, onion, and *trassie* in the oil, which should be very hot, for 5 minutes, then reduce heat and add *santen*, bay leaf, and sugar and cook until the sauce is thick. Pour over the eggs and serve as side dish for *rijsttafel*.   *Serves 4.*

SEROENDENG

This is a sort of relish that is an essential part of the *rijsttafel*. It can be bought ready-made in bottles from specialty stores, but if it is not available, the following will serve:

1 tablespoon good-quality
   vegetable oil
1 teaspoon trassie
1 onion, chopped
2 cloves garlic, crushed
1 teaspoon caraway seed
1 tablespoon ground coriander
1 tablespoon lemon juice

¼ cup brown sugar
salt to taste
2¼ cups shredded coconut (or
   the equivalent fresh grated
   coconut)
8 ounces (about 1⅔ cups)
   peanuts, roasted

Heat the oil in a heavy pan and fry the *trassie*, onion, and garlic for a few minutes. Add the caraway, coriander, lemon juice, and sugar, and season to taste with salt (be careful with salt if the peanuts are already salted). Cook for 10 minutes over moderate heat, then add the coconut and cook for 20 minutes over low heat, being careful to stir all the time; 10 minutes before serving mix in the peanuts, and serve in a shallow bowl as part of the *rijsttafel*. *Serves 4.*

VEGETABLE SALAD (*Gado-Gado*)

2 or 3 pounds (about 8 to 10
   cups) of mixed vegetables
   (such as cabbage, cauliflower,
   green beans, endive, etc.),
   some bean sprouts, and cold
   boiled potatoes
2 eggs, hard-boiled and
   quartered
deep-fried shrimp crisps

Sauce:
vegetable oil
3 cloves garlic, crushed
1 onion, finely chopped
1 teaspoon hot chili powder
3 tablespoons peanut butter
½ pint santen (see page 31)
1 tablespoon lemon juice
sugar
salt

Rough-chop the vegetables and cook briefly in boiling salted water—rather more a prolonged blanching than cooking. Drain and arrange in bowl with quartered hard-boiled eggs. Pour the sauce over the top, with deep-fried shrimp crisps for garnish.

The sauce is made by lightly frying the garlic, onion, and chili powder, then adding the remaining ingredients, including about 1 or 2 teaspoons of sugar, and bringing to a boil, then simmering for a few minutes. Allow to cool before pouring over the salad.

FRIED BANANAS   (*Pisang Goreng*)

Cut 1 large banana per person in about 4 or 5 slices lengthwise and fry in a little butter until they are golden brown. Or they may be deep-fried in hot oil or fat after being dipped in a fritter batter. Serve as side dish on *rijsttafel*.

In addition to the above dishes for the *rijsttafel*, there are numerous others made with all sorts of ingredients: Nanas Goreng, for instance, is sliced pineapple fried in batter, which really does not need a recipe. There are dishes made with liver, thin omelettes cut into long strips and served cold, omelettes with shellfish meat served hot, very small fish dipped in milk or flour and fried crisp, sweet or hotter red peppers stuffed with ground meat and seasoning, and so on.

Nasi Rames, meaning "small rice table," is the name given to the *rijsttafel* when it is served all on one plate on a bed of rice—so that the hostess may fill a guest's plate in the kitchen and save the trouble of laying out the whole table. However, this seems a shame, because part of the enjoyment of the meal is the sight of all the side dishes laid out on the table.

THE SAMBALS

Many of the relishes that are offered in small side dishes with the *rijsttafel* may be bought in specialty stores or good delicatessens, but some may also be made easily enough at home.

Sambal Oelek *(Red Chili Paste)*

This is simply a paste made by mixing 2 tablespoons of red chili peppers, minced, with ½ teaspoon each of lemon juice, grated lemon peel, oil, and salt. To make sure the paste is fine enough, it is better to make it with a pestle and mortar and put it into a glass or china pot with a lid.

Sambal Djelanteh *(Garlic and Chili Paste)*

As for Sambal Oelek, but heat the oil and fry 3 crushed cloves of garlic in it before mixing with the other ingredients. Shrimp paste may also be added.

Sambal Badjak *(Onion and Chili Paste)*

Use onion instead of garlic in the Sambal Djelanteh recipe.

Sambal Oedang *(Shrimp, Onion, and Chili Paste)*

As for Sambal Oelek, but adding half a dozen minced jumbo shrimp.

INDONESIAN FRIED RICE *(Nasi Goreng)*

This is not part of the rice table, but an Indonesian dish that is now famous all over the world. There are many different ways of preparing it; this one is my favorite.

1½ cups long-grain rice,
cooked and allowed to cool
2 onions, sliced
2 cloves garlic, crushed
½ cup butter
¾ pounds pork or other meat,
cut into small cubes
1 teaspoon chili powder
salt and pepper

soy sauce
1 pound (about 3 cups)
mixed cooked vegetables
such as peas, beans, carrots,
and the like
4 eggs
garnish of tomatoes, lettuce,
and cucumber
pickle slices

Although the ingredients list meat, this dish may be made with chicken or various sorts of fish or shellfish if desired. The rice must be previously cooked, preferably cooked the previous day and left in the refrigerator. It should also be hard-cooked (see page 30). Brown the onions and garlic in a little of the butter, then fry the cubed meat, chili powder, and seasoning for 15 minutes. Add half the rice and a good dash of soy sauce and continue cooking until the meat is tender. Keep the mixture well stirred. Add remaining rice and the cooked vegetables and mix well, cooking for another 10 minutes. Make a thin omelette with the eggs and cut into strips. Serve the rice on a dish with a lattice-work of omelette strips on the top, a garnish of tomatoes, lettuce and cucumber, and a dish of pickles on the side. *Serves 4.*

JAVANESE CABBAGE   (*Ora Arik*)

1½ cups boiled rice	*½ pound lean pork*
vegetable oil	*1 large cabbage*
2 onions, chopped	*salt and pepper*
2 cloves garlic, crushed	*2 eggs*

Rinse the rice well, soak, then cook, drain, and keep warm. Heat some oil and fry the onions and garlic, then add the pork, fry for 5 minutes, then add the cabbage, season to taste, and cook quickly until the cabbage is almost cooked. Beat the eggs lightly and stir in, frying quickly to make an omelette of the whole. Serve with rice on the side. Or this dish may be part of the *rijsttafel*. *Serves 4.*

Other Far-Eastern Rice Dishes

TRADITIONAL VIETNAMESE SOUP (*Pho*)

Pho is not strictly a rice dish, but is included here because to be really traditional the noodles should be made with rice flour. If you cannot buy such noodles, make them yourself.

Noodles:
2⅔ *cups rice flour*
good pinch salt
2 eggs

Soup:
1 pound lean beef (shin for preference)
1 marrow bone
1 large onion
star anise
1 teaspoon fresh chopped ginger

2½ pints beef stock
4 ounces good-quality raw beef, shredded
Indochinese fish (nguoc-nam) *to taste*
monosodium glutamate (optional)
juice of ½ lemon
a few scallions, chopped
few leaves of mint (apple mint if possible), chopped

Sift rice flour and salt, place beaten eggs in the center, and work them into the flour with your fingers until mixed, then add sufficient water to make a stiff dough. Roll this out as thin as possible, roll up like a jelly roll, and cut off very thin slices, which, when unrolled, may be hung out to dry like spaghetti. Dry for about 30 minutes, then boil for 7 minutes in plenty of salted water. Drain and keep hot.

Put the 1 pound beef, marrow bone, onion, quartered, a little star anise, and the chopped ginger into a stockpot with the beef stock and bring to a boil, then simmer gently for 3 hours, topping up water if it reduces too much. Strain, discard the marrow bone, and break the meat into small pieces. Into each of 6 soup bowls put a bed of noodles, covered with the cooked meat and then some of the shredded raw meat. Bring the strained soup to a boil with some of the fish sauce and a little monosodium glutamate, if desired. Stir in lemon juice, and pour soup over the noodles and meat and serve, garnished with a few chopped scallions and mint leaves. *Serves 6.*

NASI GORENG—SINGAPORE VERSION

1½ cups rice
6 ounces chicken (cooked)
6 ounces pork or ham
4 chicken livers
4 ounces button mushrooms
1 large onion
a few scallions

vegetable oil (if possible, peanut oil)
1 teaspoon hot chili powder
salt
2 eggs
2 ounces cooked shelled shrimp
chopped parsley

Cook the rice, drain, and dry. Allow to cool (or use already cooked rice). Cut the chicken and pork or ham into thin strips, and chop the chicken livers. Slice the mushrooms and chop the onion and scallions (do not mix these). Fry the onion in very hot oil without browning it, then stir in the chili, the meats, and the mushrooms. Reduce the heat and allow the meats to cook, then stir in the rice and adjust seasoning. Lightly beat the eggs and add them and the shrimp to the mixture, stirring until they are cooked. Mix in the chopped parsley and serve with the chopped scallions as a garnish. *Serves 4.*

BURMESE RICE AND COCONUT (*Ohn Hta-min*)

1¼ cups milk
1½ cups shredded coconut (or fresh if available)
2 tablespoons vegetable oil (if possible, peanut oil)

2 large onions, sliced
1½ cups rice
salt

Put the milk and coconut into a saucepan and bring to a boil. Let it stand away from the heat for 30 minutes and then squeeze the liquid out, discarding the squeezed-out coconut. The liquid is coconut milk.

Heat the oil and sauté the onions for about 5 minutes, then add the rice and cook over a high heat until the rice is brown. Stir, add salt and coconut milk (and add a little water if necessary) to bring the liquid to about 1 inch above the rice. Cover the pan and cook on low heat for 15 minutes, or until the rice is tender. *Serves 4.*

KOREAN BEEF WITH BEANS AND RICE

Marinade:	*1 cup dried kidney beans*
3 tablespoons soy sauce	*1 large onion, chopped*
1 tablespoon brown sugar	*2 cloves garlic*
3 tablespoons vegetable oil	*salt and pepper*
4 scallions, chopped	*beef stock*
a few ground sesame seeds	*3 tablespoons vegetable oil*
	½ teaspoon chili powder
1 pound frying steak	*5 ounces rice*

Mix the marinade ingredients and marinate the meat, which should be thinly sliced, overnight. Soak the kidney beans overnight, drain, add onion, garlic, salt and pepper, cover with stock (and a little water if necessary), and bring to a boil. Reduce heat, cover and simmer for 3 hours, adding a little water if needed. Make a purée of this mixture, either in an electric blender or by pressing through a sieve. Heat the oil with the chili powder, stir in the rice and bean purée, and cook 5 minutes. Put into a side dish and keep warm.

Broil the marinated meat under a very hot broiler or on a barbecue grill so that it cooks very quickly. Serve with the beans and rice mixture on the side.   *Serves 4.*

FILIPINO CRAB AND RICE   (*Alimasag*)

1 cup rice	2 eggs, beaten
½ pound chopped ham	1 teaspoon ground ginger
1 large onion, chopped	salt
2 tablespoons vegetable oil	freshly ground black pepper
3 tablespoons soy sauce	½ pound crab meat (cooked or
1 tablespoon cornstarch	canned)

Boil the rice in about 1 pint water, drain, and keep warm. Sauté the ham and onion in hot oil in a pan over medium heat for 10 minutes. Mix the soy sauce and cornstarch with about 3 or 4 tablespoons of water, stir into the ham and onion mixture until it thickens, and then gradually add the eggs, ginger, and seasoning. Cook a few minutes, then add the crab meat and cook until the crab is heated through, and serve on a bed of rice.   *Serves 4.*

LAOS BEEF WITH RICE

1 cup rice	1 tablespoon curry powder
3 tablespoons vegetable oil	1 tablespoon brown sugar
2 cups shredded coconut	1 tablespoon lemon juice
1 clove garlic, crushed	2 tablespoons soy sauce
1 small onion, chopped	salt
1 pound ground lean beef	

Boil the rice in salted boiling water, drain, and dry. Keep warm. Heat 1 tablespoon of the oil and brown the coconut in it. Drain the coconut and set aside. Put the remaining oil into the pan with the oil from the coconut and stir-fry the garlic, onion, and meat over medium heat until the meat is browned. Now add the curry powder, brown sugar, lemon juice, and soy sauce, stir in, and add 3 ounces of water. Cook for 10 minutes over low heat, stir in coconut, adjust seasoning, and serve hot on a bed of rice. *Serves 4.*

BANGKOK NESTS

1 pound rice noodles[1]
vegetable oil
1 large onion, chopped
2 cloves garlic, crushed
6 ounces chicken, shredded
6 ounces pork meat, shredded
4 tablespoons vinegar

2 tablespoons sugar
4 tablespoons soy sauce
juice of ½ lemon
anchovy paste
6 ounces shelled shrimp
bean sprouts (about 1 pound)

If the noodles are bought from a Chinese specialty shop, boil them for 2 minutes in water, then drain and dry; before they are quite dry, fashion them into 4 nest shapes.[1] Heat a little oil in a pan, lightly fry the onion and garlic, then the meats. Stir in the vinegar, sugar, soy sauce, lemon juice, and a little anchovy paste, cook for 5 minutes, add shrimp, and heat through. Cook bean sprouts in boiling salted water for 5 minutes, drain well, and mix into the meat and fish mixture, stirring in well.

Heat oil in a deep-frying pan and deep-fry each nest of noodles until golden brown and nicely crisp. Serve on individual plates with the noodle nests filled with meat and shrimp mixture. *Serves 4.*

STRAITS CHINESE FRIED RICE

Probably because Singapore and Malaysia are more exposed to foreign and particularly Western influences than China, where fried rice originated, the dish as prepared by Straits Chinese

[1] If you cannot buy rice noodles, make them as set out on page 39.

cooks assumes a more sophisticated character. There are thousands of ways of making it. This is just one.

1½ cups rice
vegetable oil (for preference,
   peanut oil)
1 large onion, chopped
1 teaspoon hot chili powder
   (or crushed fresh chili)
4 ounces each of cooked ham,
   chicken, and shelled shrimp,

and of raw chicken liver and
   raw pork, all shredded
⅔ cup sliced mushrooms
salt
2 eggs
parsley and scallions for garnish,
   chopped

Wash the rice well and cook for 15 minutes in boiling salted water, then drain and cool. Heat about 3 tablespoons of oil in a heavy pan, gently fry the onion, stir in the chili, and cook until the onion is tender but not brown. Add the uncooked meats and cook for 10 minutes over low heat. Add the mushrooms and simmer a few minutes, then the rice and the cooked meats. Stir gently and season. Make a thin omelette with the eggs and cut into narrow strips. Serve with a garnish of chopped parsley and scallions, and crisscross with the strips of egg.   *Serves 4.*

MEKONG DELTA CRAYFISH AND RICE

One of the delights of Vietnam in times of peace is the crayfish that comes from the Mekong Delta, fried in batter and accompanied by plain-boiled or savory rice, with, of course, the ubiquitous Vietnamese sauce *nguoc-nam*.

1½ cups rice
12 crayfish tails or jumbo
   shrimp
½ cup flour

½ cup cornstarch
1 large egg
very cold water
vegetable oil

Since you are unlikely to buy Mekong Delta crayfish in America, settle for jumbo shrimp, uncooked if possible (fresh or frozen). Boil rice, drain, and keep warm. Shell shrimp except for the tail shell, devein, and slice almost through across the shrimp in two or three places so that they may be flattened with the side of a knife. Make a very light batter with the flour, cornstarch, egg, and water from the refrigerator. Take each shrimp by the tail shell, dip into the batter, and drop into very hot oil and deep-fry. The batter should be so light that cooking to a golden brown will take almost no time and the fritter around the shrimp should be gossamer-thin. *Serves 4.*

SIAMESE SUBGUM

1½ *cups rice*	8 *ounces cooked chicken meat,*
3 *eggs*	*diced*
salt and pepper	8 *ounces cooked ham, diced*
vegetable oil	¾ *cup frozen peas, cooked*
3 *onions, chopped*	*soy sauce*

Cook the rice and drain well. Beat the eggs only slightly with about ¼ teaspoon salt and fry them in a tablespoon of oil, stirring well so that they are a sort of scrambled omelette when cooked. Set aside. Heat a little more oil, cook onions for 1 minute, then add the cooked rice and stir until the rice and onions are well mixed and heated through. Mix in chicken, ham, and peas, and add salt and pepper to taste. Heat through again, mix in scrambled eggs, and serve with soy sauce either separate or stirred in (about 2 tablespoons) just before serving. *Serves 4.*

Rice with the Indians

When you look at cookery in India (I mean, broadly, the subcontinent far beyond the borders of modern India), you may wonder how food ever gets to the mouths of Indian families through the maze of religious restrictions, caste taboos, and the normal shortage in some parts of the country of what we would regard as essential foods. Yet the Indians do eat, and rice is the basis of their diet, as it is with so many Eastern peoples. Very little food is prepared that does not have rice with it or is not served with rice as accompaniment.

Members of some religious groups may not eat pork, others regard the cow as sacred and therefore cannot eat beef; fat from either animal is also denied to certain groups, and there are others who must not eat fish. Orthodox members of some groups may eat only food that has been prepared under certain conditions and according to certain rites, roughly similar to the Jewish idea of kosher food. Members of certain castes, despite efforts to wipe out the caste system, are restricted to food prepared by certain other castes, and so on. Rice seems to be the least affected food of all.

But rice by itself, like Italian pasta or plain dry bread, is a rather tasteless staff of life. So the Indians, like other peoples, developed highly-flavored foods to go with it and make it more palatable, and so curry was born, to become as indispensable to the Indian diet as tomato to the Italian or sausage to the German. There is probably no greater individualist in the world than the Indian cook, who believes that cooking emanates from the Supreme Deity and should be carried out as a holy rite, according to certain rules that the cook carries in his head. Recipes, therefore, are often apt to be vague and, in any case, similar dishes may be prepared in very different ways in different parts of India. So for the purposes of this book, various dishes that include or go with rice have been standardized, so to speak, so that they can be made in Western kitchens. Some of the materials may sound exotic, but there are now Asian shops in the United States from which these items may be obtained, or replaced by a handy substitute.

The Indian custom with rice is to wash it well before beginning to cook it. This undoubtedly stems from the fact that in many parts of India the rice might well be dirty, or contain much foreign matter, whereas in America what you buy will most likely have been washed already. But if you wish to follow the Indian style, choose Patna or long-grain rice and wash it at least four times in cold water. In some places the rice is then left in water for an hour or two before being drained and cooked. The Indian style is to throw the washed rice into plenty of boiling, salted water, something in the order of 7 pints of water for 2 cups of rice, in a very large saucepan so that the water can be kept boiling as the rice cooks. For 2 cups the cooking time should be 12 minutes. It is cooked if it is tender when pressed between thumb and forefinger. Drain it in a colander and pour a cupful of warm water through it to separate the grains; after draining another few minutes it should still be hot enough to serve.

Another method frequently used in India is to wash and soak the rice, drain it, place it in a pan with a tight-fitting lid, add a little salt, and cover the rice with boiling water to an inch above the rice. After simmering for 25 minutes, with the lid tightly on, it should have absorbed all the liquid and be tender and almost dry.

SAVORY RICES

The Indians have a number of savory rices that are served with various dishes. Here are some of the most popular ones:

COCONUT RICE

3 ounces ghee[1]
2 good-sized onions, finely
   chopped

1½ cups Patna or long-grain rice
2 pints coconut milk[2]
salt

Heat the ghee and fry the onions gently, without letting them brown. Add the rice after it has been well washed, soaked, and drained, the coconut milk, and extra water if required to ensure that the rice is covered and the liquid an inch above it. Salt to taste and simmer with lid on over low heat until liquid is absorbed and the rice well cooked. It should be stirred once or twice during cooking, which should take about 25 minutes. *Note:* unlike some other forms of rice, the grains in this dish will stick together. *Serves 4.*

RICE WITH LENTILS (*also called Kedgeree or Kitcheree*)

1½ cups long-grain rice
1 cup lentils
1 large onion, finely chopped
3 ounces clarified butter (ghee)
pinch of ground cloves

¼ teaspoon each powdered
   cumin and cardamom
1 teaspoon turmeric powder
½ teaspoon ground cinnamon
salt and pepper

Wash and soak rice. Soak lentils for 1 hour. Drain both rice and lentils. Fry onion gently in clarified butter with spices, but without browning onion. Add rice, stir, then add lentils; cook over moderate heat for 10 minutes, stirring, then add boiling water to cover up

---

[1] Ghee is simply clarified butter (made by melting butter in a pan, stirring, and then cooling, so that impurities drop to the bottom and allow the clarified butter to be taken off the top).

[2] Coconut milk is not the milk of coconuts but is made by steeping freshly grated or shredded coconut in boiling water, then squeezing out the coconut shreds into the liquor after it has soaked for an hour or more.

to 1 inch above rice, cover, and simmer for about 25 to 30 minutes until cooked and almost dry. Season to taste. Stir, leave on very low heat without lid for about 5 minutes, then serve. *Serves 4.*

Yellow Rice

Proceed exactly as for Rice with Lentils, but using 2 cups rice and eliminating lentils, and adding 1 crushed clove of garlic when frying the onion.

Onion Rice

Fry the required amount of cold cooked rice in a pan in clarified butter with finely chopped onions and garlic and some freshly ground black pepper.

CURRIES

Curry goes with rice as chips go with fish, sauerkraut with frankfurters, a Bolognese sauce with spaghetti, or mint sauce with lamb. But there are thousands of different types of curry, and if an accurate survey were made it would probably confirm that no two Indian chefs make it the same way. Each has his own very particular idea of the ingredients, and since there are about a dozen popular ingredients, you might try working out how many different permutations within a few ounces of each ingredient you could get from them. However, for practical purposes, there are accepted combinations of the main spices for currying various foods. The Indians usually make them up in sufficient quantity to cook only one meal. You could easily do the same, or you could buy a few different types of curry powder, commonly available from various delicatessens and Asian shops, already made up. If you choose to make your own a coffee grinder will help, but don't use it when it smells of coffee, and don't leave the taste of spices in it or your next cup of coffee will have a slightly odd taste, to say the least.

The main ingredients of all the various curries are coriander, turmeric, cumin, chili, mustard seed, ginger, pepper, and fenugreek. It is better to grind your own seeds, but all can be bought easily in powdered form. Some forms of curry are improved if, when making the curry powder, you finish off by mixing it into a paste with a little vinegar or lemon juice (the Indians use tamarind juice, if you can find any here). Curry in paste form, according to some cooks, imparts its flavor better to the food being curried. It is certainly easier to use.

The following are some of the main types of curry dishes with rice and suggested variations of the curry formula for each type. It will be noticed that four ingredients are predominant: coriander, turmeric, cumin, and chili powder. It is the last-named that makes the curry really hot (or not so hot) as Westerners understand the word, so that you may alter the quantity of this ingredient to suit your own taste.

In these recipes the curry mixture is given in proportions of ingredients so that enough of the mixture for several curries may be made up at once if so desired. Roughly speaking, if you use a level teaspoon as a unit, the mixtures will make enough for a curry for 4 persons, but some may like more or less of the mixture.

CURRIED EGGS WITH RICE

1½ *cups long-grain rice*
1 *onion, finely chopped*
1 *clove garlic* (*optional*)
1 *tablespoon clarified butter*
1¼ *pints stock or coconut milk*
   (*see page 48*)
6 *hard-boiled eggs*
juice of 1 lemon

salt

Curry mixture proportions:
2 *parts coriander*
1 *part turmeric*
½ *part each cumin, chili, and*
   ginger

Boil rice, dry, and keep warm. Fry the onion and garlic (if used) in the butter until the onion is browned. Add the curry mixture, stir in well, and fry for 5 minutes. Add a few spoonfuls of stock, stir well, and cook for another 5 minutes, then add sufficient stock to make the curry gravy as thick as desired; cook for 10 minutes, then add the hard-boiled eggs, halved, quartered, or thick-sliced as desired, and cook for 5 minutes more. Season with lemon juice and salt to taste and serve with rice on the side. *Serves 4.*

CURRIED SHRIMP (OR OTHER SHELLFISH) AND RICE

1½ cups long-grain rice

2 onions, finely chopped

1 clove garlic (optional)

1 tablespoon clarified butter

1 tablespoon tomato paste

1¼ cups coconut milk (see page 48)

salt

2 tomatoes, chopped

½ pound shelled shrimp

Curry mixture proportions:

3 parts coriander

1 part turmeric

½ part each cumin, chili, and mustard seed

Boil the rice, dry, and keep warm. Fry the onions and garlic in the butter until brown, then add curry, tomato paste, and a couple of spoons of coconut milk (stock may be used if no coconut milk is available) and simmer for 10 minutes. Season to taste with salt, then mix in the chopped tomato and shrimp and cook gently for 5 minutes more, thinning out with more stock until the required consistency is reached. If the curry is still too thick when all the coconut milk has been used up, add a little water or stock. Serve with rice on the side. *Serves 4.*

CURRIED FISH AND RICE

1½ cups long-grain rice
vinegar or lemon juice
½ onion, chopped finely
1 clove garlic, crushed
2 tablespoons clarified butter
1¼ cups coconut milk (see
    page 48)
1½ pounds firm white fish,
    in small steaks or pieces

salt

Curry mixture proportions:
3 parts coriander
1 part each turmeric and cumin
½ part each chili, fenugreek,
    and ginger

Boil rice, dry, and keep warm. Mix as much as you require of the curry powder with a little vinegar or lemon juice to make a paste. Fry the onion and garlic in the butter, add the curry mixture, cook a few minutes, then add the remainder of the coconut milk (or stock), stir well, add the fish, and simmer gently until the fish is cooked. Season to taste and serve with rice on the side.   *Serves 4.*

CHICKEN CURRY AND RICE: 1

1½ cups long-grain rice
1 large onion, chopped
1 clove garlic (optional)
¼ cup clarified butter
1 medium-sized chicken, cut
    into 8 parts
1¼ pints stock
salt

Curry mixture proportions:
3 parts coriander
1 part each turmeric, cumin,
    and mustard seed
½ part each chili and ginger

pappadoms (optional)

Boil the rice, dry, and keep warm. Brown the onion and garlic in the butter, add the curry mixture, and stir for 3 minutes. Add the chicken pieces and fry until brown, then add the stock and simmer until the chicken is quite tender. This should take about 30 minutes. A little water may be added if the curry is too thick. Season to taste. Serve with rice on the side, and pappadoms if desired. *Serves 4.*

CHICKEN CURRY AND RICE: 2

Exactly as for (1), but using the following curry mixture:

3 parts coriander
2 parts shredded coconut
1 part each turmeric and mustard seed
½ part each cumin, chili, and black pepper
¼ part fenugreek

DUCK CURRY AND RICE

As for chicken, but use these proportions in the curry mixture:

6 parts coriander
4 parts turmeric
½ part each cumin, chili, fenugreek, and ginger

The same recipe as for duck may be used for various game birds, goose, turkey, etc.

CURRIED PORK WITH RICE

1½ cups long-grain rice
2 onions, chopped
1 clove garlic, crushed
¼ cup clarified butter
2 tablespoons chopped fresh
   ginger
pinch ground cloves
pinch cinnamon

1 pound lean pork, cut in
   1-inch squares
1¼ pints stock
salt

Curry mixture proportions:
3 parts coriander
1 part turmeric
½ part each cumin and chili

Boil rice, dry, and keep warm. Fry onions and garlic in butter until brown, add ginger, cook for 2 minutes, add good pinches ground cloves and cinnamon, cook for 2 minutes more, add pieces of pork, and fry until browned. Add a little stock to moisten, then add curry mixture, stir well, and cook for a few minutes. Add remaining stock and simmer until the pork is tender, for about 25 minutes. Season to taste and serve with rice on the side.   *Serves 4.*

CURRIED BEEF WITH RICE: 1

1½ cups long-grain rice
¼ cup clarified butter
3 onions, chopped
1 clove garlic, crushed
1½ pounds lean beef
2 tomatoes, chopped
1¼ pints stock
salt

Curry mixture proportions:
3 parts coriander
1 part turmeric
½ part cumin
¼ part each black pepper,
   chili, mustard seed, and
   fenugreek

lemon quarters
mango chutney

Boil rice, dry, and keep warm. Heat the butter and fry the onion and garlic until brown, mix in the curry powder, cook for 3 minutes, then add beef and fry for 5 minutes over medium heat, stirring and turning meat. Add the tomato and cook for 2 minutes, then add the stock and simmer, covered, until the meat is cooked and the gravy sufficiently thick, for about ½ hour. If the curry is too thick, add a few spoonfuls of water. Season to taste and serve with quarters of lemon, mango chutney, and rice on the side. *Serves 4.*

CURRIED BEEF WITH RICE: 2

As above, but eliminating tomato and using these curry mixture proportions:

3 parts coriander
½ part each turmeric, cumin, and chili
¼ part each pepper and ginger

CURRIED LAMB AND RICE

1½ cups long-grain rice	*salt*
1½ pounds lean lamb	
2 onions, sliced	Curry mixture proportions:
1 clove garlic, crushed	*3 parts coriander*
¼ cup clarified butter	*1¼ parts turmeric*
1¼ pints coconut milk (see	*½ part each cumin, black*
page 48) or stock	*pepper, and chili*

Boil the rice, dry, and keep warm. Cut the meat into squares of 1 inch or slightly less. Fry the onion and garlic in butter, add the curry mixture, cook for a few minutes, then add meat and fry for

5 minutes. Gradually add coconut milk or stock and simmer until meat is tender, adding a few spoonfuls of water if curry becomes too thick. Season with salt. Serve with rice on the side. *Serves 4.*

VEGETABLE CURRY AND RICE

1½ *cups long-grain rice*
1 *onion, chopped*
1 *clove garlic, crushed*
2 *tablespoons clarified butter*
1½ *pounds (about 5 to 6 cups)*
   mixed prepared vegetables
   (peas, beans, carrots, turnips,
   etc.)
stock

salt

Vegetable curry proportions:
3 *parts coriander*
1 *part turmeric*
½ *part each cumin, chili,*
   ginger, and mustard seed
¼ *part fenugreek*

Boil rice, dry, and keep warm. Fry onion and garlic in butter until brown, add curry powder, fry for 3 minutes, add vegetables, fry for 3 minutes; then add stock and simmer until vegetables are cooked. Do not overcook them: they should be firm but tender in the curry. Season to taste and serve with rice on the side, or as an accompaniment to other dishes with rice. *Serves 4.*

OTHER CURRIES

Vindaloo curries are a little more like stews than ordinary curry since they are more liquid. But they are also much hotter (by increasing the amount of chili) and are made from rich foods like geese, duck, fat pork, etc. They are popular in southern India.

Dry curries are made by making a paste of a strong curry mixture and working it into cut-up meat or poultry, which is then fried in clarified butter.

Korma dishes are from the north of India, very spicy but not hot; most are marinated first in sour curd.

Koftas are a sort of spiced meat ball cooked in a curry sauce.

PILAFS WITH RICE

Like most countries east of the Mediterranean, India has a wide variety of pilafs made with rice. The rice is well soaked, then drained, then fried lightly in clarified butter, with onion and garlic, and spiced with cardamom, cinnamon, and cloves, colored with saffron, and mixed with nuts and raisins. Following is a basic recipe for the pilaf rice, which can be used with all sorts of main ingredients.

*2 cups long-grain or **Patna** rice*	*8 cloves*
1 large onion, chopped	*8 cardamom seeds*
2 cloves garlic, crushed	*pinch saffron*
¾ cup clarified butter	*salt and pepper*
1 teaspoon ground cinnamon	*⅓ cup blanched almonds*
½ teaspoon ground allspice	*4 ounces raisins*

Wash the rice under running water for some time, then soak in a large bowl of cold water for a couple of hours. Drain. Fry the onion and garlic in ½ cup butter for a few minutes, until translucent but not brown, then add the spices. Cook for 2 minutes, add rice, and cook for 5 minutes before adding saffron dissolved in ½ cup water, and about 2½ pints of boiling water (or enough to rise about 1 inch above the top of the rice). Season to taste, close lid of the pan tightly, and bring to a boil, then reduce heat and simmer very gently until rice is almost dry, for about 25 to 30 minutes. Fry the blanched almonds and the raisins in remaining ¼ cup butter and empty the pan into the rice; stir to mix fruit, nuts, butter, and rice well together.   *Serves 5 to 6.*

Using the basic pilaf recipe, the Indians prepare a wide range of dishes based on meat, poultry, shrimp, vegetables, and so on. In most cases the meat, vegetables, or whatever is cooked in stock until tender, then small pieces of it worked into the pilaf rice and mixed up.

A biriani in the luxurious Moghlai style, for instance, would be a dish of richly cooked chicken in spices and extra butter, worked into the pilaf rice with a variety of nuts, dates, and other fruit, and then put into the oven for further cooking.

JEWISH CURRIED RICE AND NUTS

Jews in India often cook a dish of their traditional curried nuts and rice.

1 teaspoon curry powder (or paste)	*1½ cups rice*
	¼ cup raisins
pinch of saffron	*1 cup chopped walnuts*
salt	*vegetable oil*

Put 2½ pints water into a saucepan with the curry powder (or paste), saffron, and a teaspoon of salt. Wash rice well, drain, and place in saucepan with curry and saffron. Cook for 20 minutes over moderate heat, drain well, and keep warm. Wash raisins and drain; sauté the chopped walnuts in a little oil, then add raisins and cook for a few minutes. Drain raisins and nuts and scatter over the rice on a serving dish, and pour a little of the oil in which they were fried over the rice as well.   *Serves 4.*

INDIAN RICE PUDDING

1½ *cups rice*
½ *teaspoon salt*
good pinch saffron
1 *cup sugar*
¾ *cup butter*
2 *cardamom seeds*
3 *cloves*

1 *cup chopped mixed nuts*
  (*including almond,*
  pistachio, cashew, etc.)
1 *ounce raisins*
juice of 1 lemon
½ *cup heavy cream, whipped*

Boil the rice in salted water with pinch of saffron for 10 minutes, then drain. Make a syrup by boiling the sugar in 1 pint water for a couple of minutes until the sugar is dissolved. Put the butter into a heavy large pan, heat, add cardamom seeds and cloves, simmer for 10 minutes, then add most of the syrup and bring to a boil. Add rice, cook for 10 minutes. When most of the butter has been absorbed, add the nuts, raisins, and lemon juice. Increase the heat for a few minutes, then reduce to a simmer until the rice is tender, if necessary adding the remainder of the syrup. Stir frequently. Allow to cool slightly; top with whipped cream when serving.   *Serves 6.*

Rice in Pakistan

BIRIANI OF CHICKEN

You could call a biriani a sort of pilaf (or a pilaf a sort of biriani, for that matter), but there are some essential differences in preparation as they are cooked in Pakistan. For our purposes the main thing about biriani is that the rice undergoes some cooking before it is put with the meat (or, in this case, chicken) and the meat itself undergoes quite a considerable culinary operation before it is mixed with the rice. It is, in fact, a sort of three-stage operation, as will be seen below.

1½ *cups long-grain rice*	2 *tablespoons chopped fresh*
2 *onions, sliced*	*ginger*
2 *cloves garlic, crushed*	¼ *teaspoon turmeric*
¾ *cup butter*	2 *8-ounce containers plain*
good pinch saffron	*yogurt*
3 *cloves*	1 *medium-sized chicken,*
3 *to 4 cardamom seeds*	*jointed into 8 pieces*
salt	1 *tablespoon chopped*
a few peppercorns	*almonds*
1 *stick cinnamon*	2 *tablespoons raisins*

The first stage consists of cooking the rice: soak the rice for several hours in cold water, then drain it. Fry the onions and 1 clove of garlic in ¼ cup butter until the onions are browned and crisp; take out the onions and set aside. Now put the rice, pinch of saffron, the cloves and cardamom seeds roughly crushed, and salt and pepper to taste into the pan and fry, stirring, until the rice is coated and the spices well mixed in. Add about 1 pint boiling water and cinnamon stick and cook quickly. By the time the water has disappeared the rice will be about half cooked. Remove cinnamon stick and set rice aside.

The second stage consists of making a marinade for the meat, marinating it, and cooking it. Crush the remaining clove garlic together with the ginger and turmeric and mix with 1 container of the yogurt. Marinate the chicken pieces in this for at least an hour, turning once or twice. Heat the remainder of the butter in another pan and cook the chicken over high heat for a few minutes, and then over a gentle heat until the chicken is cooked.

The third stage mixes all the ingredients and finishes the cooking. Choose a fireproof dish with a lid, put half the rice in the bottom, and over this the marinade, if any is left. Lay the chicken joints on this and sprinkle over them the almonds, raisins, and cooked onions. Spread the other half of the rice over this and the second container of yogurt over the top. Cover and put in a moderate oven (350° F.) until the rice is completely cooked and has absorbed the yogurt.

This is Moghlai biriani, the Moghlai dishes being the rich ones from the north. More or less butter and more or less rich ingredients can be used, according to taste. The Pakistanis often use the dish for celebrations like weddings and so on, and in these cases it is served on silver dishes with very expensive trimmings. *Serves 4.*

Other birianis may be made by substituting lamb, etc., for the chicken but otherwise cooked in the same way.

PAKISTANI CHICKEN PILAF

¾ *cup clarified butter*	1 *medium-sized chicken,*
1 *clove garlic, crushed*	*jointed into 8 pieces*
2 *large onions, sliced*	1½ *cups rice*
2 *sticks cinnamon*	*salt and pepper*
a few cardamom seeds,	2½ *pints chicken stock*
crushed	

Heat the butter in a heavy pan, fry the garlic, onions, cinnamon, and cardamom for 2 minutes; remove the onions and keep hot. Add the chicken pieces to the pan and fry until golden. Return the onions and add the rice to the pan, season, and fry for 5 minutes. Add the stock, making sure that the rice is covered to a depth of 1 inch.

Cook very gently over low heat with the lid tightly closed on the pan for at least 30 minutes, then finish off in a slow oven (300° F.) until the rice is virtually dry.   *Serves 4.*

KOFTA PILAF

1½ *cups rice*
1 *pound ground meat* (*beef, lamb, etc.*)
1 *large onion, finely chopped*
1 *egg*
1 *tablespoon flour*
¼ *teaspoon each ground turmeric, coriander, mustard, cumin, ginger, and red chili powder*

¾ *cup clarified butter*
1 *clove garlic, crushed*
2 *pints stock*
pinch of saffron
⅓ *cup roasted almonds*
⅓ *cup raisins*
salt
1 *8-ounce container plain yogurt*

Wash the rice and leave to soak in cold water about 2 hours. Drain well.

Koftas are a sort of meat ball. Mix the meat, onion, egg, flour, and spices and shape into balls about the size of a walnut. Heat ¼ cup butter in heavy pan, add the garlic, and fry the meat balls until cooked.

Heat the remaining butter in a sauté pan, add the rice, and fry gently until the grains are translucent. Add the stock, with a pinch of saffron, the almonds and the raisins, and bring to a boil, then reduce heat and simmer very gently, with lid tightly closed, until the liquid has been absorbed. Season to taste. Mix in the koftas and serve hot. Serve yogurt on the side.   *Serves 4.*

Rice in the Middle East

RICE AND LENTIL PORRIDGE (*Adas Majroush*)

A porridge-style dish of lentils and rice is made in some Arab
countries, but it is strictly for strong stomachs.

2 cups lentils, crushed
1½ cups rice
salt and pepper

3 cloves garlic
vegetable oil

Wash the lentils and rice and bring to a boil in a saucepan with
about 1¼ pints of water and salt and pepper to taste. Reduce heat
and simmer gently until the cereals become a thick porridge. Chop
the garlic and fry in a little oil. Then, when the porridge has
cooled a little, pour the oil and garlic over it. *Serves 4.*

FISH AND RICE LAYERS

1 medium-sized cauliflower
vegetable oil
1 pound smoked haddock or
   cod
milk

1½ cups rice
salt and pepper
1 8-ounce container plain
   yogurt

Blanch the cauliflower, break into flowerets, and dry, then fry in
oil until half cooked. Poach the haddock or cod in a little milk;
drain. Fry the rice in a little cooking oil until it has changed to a
brown color; cover with water and simmer until the water is absorbed. In an ovenproof casserole place successive layers of rice,
fish, rice, cauliflower, and rice, season to taste, and bake for 15
minutes in a hot (450° F.) oven. When serving spread the
yogurt over each helping. *Serves 4.*

GROUND MEAT KEBABS WITH RICE
(*Kabab Matchoun eb Ruz*)

1½ *cups rice*	4 *tablespoons chopped parsley*
1 *pound ground beef* (*or other uncooked meat*)	*salt and pepper*
	ground nutmeg
1 *large onion, finely chopped*	*vegetable oil*

Cook rice, drain, and keep warm. Make a mixture of the ground meat, onion, parsley, and seasoning of salt, pepper, and nutmeg, with just enough oil to bind the mixture. Shape it into small balls and thread these onto kebab skewers and grill over charcoal at a barbecue, or under the broiler in the kitchen. Serve hot on a bed of rice.   *Serves 4.*

TRIPE STUFFED WITH RICE AND BEEF

1 *piece of tripe* (*about 1 pound, uncut*)	1 *large onion, chopped*
	vegetable oil
½ *pound ground beef*	*salt and pepper*
1 *cup rice*	*ground nutmeg*

Boil the tripe gently for 2 hours. Drain and place it on a chopping board. Make a mixture of the meat, rice, onion, a generous tablespoon of oil, and salt, pepper, and nutmeg to taste and put the mixture in the center of the tripe. Wrap the tripe around the mixture in bag form and sew it with heavy thread to keep its shape. Heat some oil in a heavy saucepan and brown the bag of tripe all over, then cover with water, which should be boiling, bring to a boil again, reduce heat, and simmer until the water is almost all absorbed. Remove thread from tripe and serve hot.   *Serves 5 to 6.*

PILAFS

Pilafs come in all sorts of styles—meat, fish, or vegetable—in the Middle East, which may be where they were invented. Methods of cooking pilafs vary in different parts of the area, but basically they are the same: the rice is cooked in stock, so that the rice absorbs the savory element in the liquid. In some cases the rice is fried first, in other cases it is not. Vegetables are usually cooked with the rice, but in some of the more elaborate pilafs the flavor in the rice comes from the stock, with meat, poultry, or, for instance, shellfish, added when cooking is almost complete.

The possible number of pilafs is infinite: use your own initiative to find the particular savory type you like best. Meanwhile, here are a few from the Middle East that you can try.

BOSPORUS SHRIMP PILAF

*1 pound raw large shrimp (or
    ½ pound cooked and
    shelled)
¼ cup butter
2 cloves garlic, crushed
1 onion, chopped
2 tomatoes, chopped
2 stalks celery, chopped*

*1½ cups rice
good pinch saffron (turmeric
    if no saffron available)
1¼ pints stock (shrimp
    or fish)
salt and pepper
1 lemon
chopped parsley*

If the shrimp are cooked and peeled, heat the butter and fry the garlic, onion, tomatoes, and celery. If the shrimp are raw, peel them and fry gently for 3 minutes before adding the onions, etc. (In this case use the heads and shells to make stock.) Wash the rice in water until the water is clear, drain well, and add to the pan, with a pinch of saffron to color it, stir well, then cover with the fish stock. Simmer gently until all the liquid is absorbed. A few minutes before serving add the shrimp to the rice, season to taste, and heat through before serving. Garnish with lemon slices and chopped parsley.   *Serves 4.*

FISH PILAF

1½ cups rice	vegetable oil
1¼ pints fish stock	3 hard-boiled eggs
1 pound smoked cod	salt and pepper
1 large onion, chopped	1 2-ounce can anchovies

Cook the rice in the pilaf fashion (see page 65) and keep warm. Poach the smoked fish, cool, and shred or cut into 1-inch squares. Fry onion gently in a little oil, add fish and chopped eggs only long enough to heat them, season to taste, then mix the contents of the pan in with the rice, garnish with anchovies, and serve. *Serves 4.*

JEWISH CHICKEN PILAF (*Pillao*)

vegetable oil	1 pound boned chicken meat,
2 onions, sliced	cut into cubes
2 large carrots, diced	salt and pepper
1½ cups rice	

Heat 3 or 4 tablespoons oil in a heavy saucepan, add onions and carrots, and fry until brown. Add the rice, stir well, cook for 5 minutes, add chicken, and cook for 5 minutes more. Add 1¼ pints boiling water, cover pan with foil and lid, and simmer very gently over low heat for 30 minutes, without removing lid. Season to taste before serving.   *Serves 4.*

ARABIC PILAF (*Ruz eb jaj*)

1 *pound boned chicken,*
  cubed
3 *tablespoons vegetable oil*
1½ *cups rice*

salt and pepper
pine nuts or pignolias (or
  chopped almonds)

This dish can be made with cooked chicken. If uncooked, stew the chicken in water with a little salt until tender. Heat oil in a heavy pan, add rice and salt and pepper, and cook over moderate heat until the rice is browned. Add boned chicken meat; add water to the stock in which the chicken was cooked to make it up to 1¼ pints; bring this to a boil and add to the rice and chicken. The mixture must not be stirred. Cover with lid, simmer over gentle heat until the liquid has been absorbed, and then a few minutes more until a sort of golden crust has formed on the bottom of the rice. Dry-fry the nuts and sprinkle over top before serving. *Serves 4.*

STUFFED VEGETABLES (*Khoudra Mahshi*)

Arabs are fond of vegetables such as zucchini, eggplant, and so on stuffed with a beef and rice mixture. The same recipe will apply whatever vegetable is used.

1½ *cups rice*
¾ *pound beef or other meat*
1 *large onion, chopped*
chopped parsley

salt and pepper
vegetable oil
1 *large eggplant per person*

Make a stuffing by mixing the rice, meat, chopped onion, parsley, salt, and pepper and frying it in a little oil until there is no pink left in the meat. Halve the eggplants lengthwise and scoop out the flesh, leaving the shell of the vegetable intact. Chop the flesh and mix it with the stuffing, fry for 5 minutes more, then divide the filling among the eggplant shells. Place in a casserole, cover with water, and simmer gently until all the liquid is absorbed. This may be done in a moderate oven (350° F.). *Serves 4.*

STUFFED VINE LEAVES—JEWISH VERSION
(*Alleh gefen menna'im*)

1½ cups rice	*parsley, chopped*
1 large onion, chopped	*fresh mint, chopped*
1¼ cups vegetable oil	*20 vine leaves, blanched*
1 teaspoon anise seed	*juice of 2 lemons*
salt and pepper	

Wash the rice under running water, drain well. Fry the onion in a little oil until browned, then add rice, which should be dry. Add anise and seasoning and fry a few minutes, then add 2 tablespoons chopped parsley and a handful of fresh mint, chopped. Cook for a few minutes, remove from heat, and divide contents of the pan among the 20 vine leaves. Wrap each one like a parcel, squeeze it out and then lay it in a shallow roasting pan with remaining cooking oil, the lemon juice, and enough hot water to cover the leaves and their contents. Cover with a lid or foil. Bring to a boil, then reduce the heat and simmer for about 1½ hours or until cooked and most of the liquor has been absorbed.

This version of this dish makes an excellent vegetable accompaniment to various meats. *Serves 4.*

MIDDLE EASTERN STUFFED PEPPERS

8 *green peppers*	½ *pound ground beef (or*
1 *large onion, chopped*	*other meat)*
vegetable oil	*sugar*
½ *cup rice*	*salt and pepper*
2 *tablespoons chopped fresh*	1 8-*ounce can tomatoes*
mint	2 *tablespoons tomato paste*
2 *tablespoons chopped parsley*	½ *cup sour cream*

Remove tops from peppers, core, seed, and blanch. Fry the onion in about 5 tablespoons oil, add rice, fry for 5 minutes, then add the herbs, meat, a little sugar, seasoning, and tomatoes; cook for 5 minutes, mixing well. Spoon equal quantities of this mixture into each pepper, pack them into a fireproof casserole or saucepan, replace the tops on the peppers, add tomato paste (a little on top of each pepper), and cover with hot water. Bring to a boil, reduce heat, and simmer gently for 30 minutes. Serve with a little sour cream on each pepper. *Serves 4.*

ARABIC STUFFED PEPPERS *(Filfel Akhdar Mahshi)*

6 *medium-sized green peppers*	6 *large green olives, chopped*
1 *cup long-grain rice*	1 *tablespoon almonds, skinned*
¾ *pound ground beef*	*and chopped*
or lamb	½ *teaspoon cinnamon*
2 *onions, chopped*	2 *teaspoons coriander*
2 *tomatoes (or an 8-ounce can),*	*salt and pepper*
chopped	1¼ *pints stock*

Slice the tops from the peppers and keep for lids; remove cores and seeds and blanch in boiling water for 3 or 4 minutes. Drain and stand upright in a casserole dish. Mix rice, meat, onions, tomatoes, olives, nuts, spices, and seasoning, and fill the peppers, replacing the tops. Cover with stock and cook in a moderate oven (350° F.) for 1 hour, or until rice and meat are cooked. This dish should be basted several times during cooking.   *Serves 6.*

IMAM BAILDI WITH RICE

Imam Baildi, or the Fainting Imam, is a very well known Turkish dish. Here is an interesting version using rice.

¾ cup rice	2 tablespoons chopped parsley
4 medium-sized eggplants	salt and pepper
4 medium-sized onions	sugar
2 cloves garlic, crushed	olive oil (up to about 1¼ cups)
4 large tomatoes (or 1 16-ounce can)	1¼ cups stock (or tomato juice)
	juice of 1 lemon

Cook the rice, drain, and dry. Blanch the eggplants in boiling water for about 8 minutes, dry, and cut in halves lengthwise. Spoon out some of the pulp and discard. Make a stuffing by gently frying the onions, garlic, tomatoes, chopped parsley, and seasoning with a pinch or two of sugar in good-quality olive oil. When the vegetables are soft, mix in the rice and divide this filling among the 8 halves of eggplant. Now lay these in a well-buttered casserole dish and pour the remainder of the olive oil over them. Add the stock and lemon juice to the dish and cook in a preheated moderate oven (350° F.) for 45 to 60 minutes, cool, and put in the refrigerator to be served cold. You may vary the amount of olive oil used to suit your taste in the finished dish (the Imam is said to have fainted at the amount his wife used), but do not try using other oil or fats.   *Serves 4.*

MAHALLEBI

1½ pints milk
2 ounces ground rice
¼ cup cornstarch
¼ cup sugar

vanilla or other flavoring
  extract
cream or yogurt

Use a little of the cold milk to make a paste of the ground rice and cornstarch. Heat the rest of the milk, add the sugar, and pour into the rice and cornstarch, return to the saucepan, and boil until the mixture thickens, stirring continually. Add the flavoring and chill. Serve cold with cream or yogurt. *Serves 4.*

Rice with the Italians

It is often said that rice is to the northern Italian what spaghetti and other pastas are to the southerner. Be that as it may, there is something special about the northern rice dishes, particularly if they are cooked with Italian rice, which produces a creamy, moist dish rather than the dry pilaf type favored farther east. Italian rice will cost a little more than the ordinary long-grain type, but it is worth it if you can buy it. If not, use long-grain as a substitute. Unlike people in some other countries, the Italians favor stock, or at least water flavored with lemon or a little wine, for cooking their rice, rather than plain water. They do not believe in washing the rice first, but instead they put it straight into boiling liquid—plenty of liquid so that it has room to move, not unlike the way they cook spaghetti and macaroni. The liquid should be kept at a fast boil for about 15 minutes and then the rice tested to see if it is *al dente*, that is, tender but not soft. If it is cooked, it is drained well, then put into a buttered pan and dried in a cool oven. Unlike some people who say you should never stir rice, the Italians run a fork through it several times while it is drying in the oven just to make sure the grains do not stick together.

As the following recipes illustrate, a lot of Italians fry rice gently in a little oil before adding the stock to cook it. Generally 2 cups of rice will absorb as much as 2½ pints of stock and swell to three times its size in the process of cooking and absorbing the liquid.

The great dishes of northern Italy are the *risottos* (or rice dishes) and here is a selection.

RISOTTO MILANESE

½ *cup butter*
2 *ounces bone marrow (if obtainable)*
2 *onions, chopped*
1½ *cups Italian rice*
4 *tablespoons white wine*

1 *clove garlic, crushed*
salt and pepper
2 *pints chicken stock*
pinch saffron
grated Parmesan

Melt ¼ cup butter in a heavy pan or stockpot. Chop bone marrow and add, with the onions, to pan. When these are brown, add the rice and cook for 15 minutes over a moderate heat, stirring so that all the rice is well coated. Add wine, garlic, seasoning, and 1¼ cups stock. Simmer gently, adding more stock when the rice begins to dry: about 20 minutes should be sufficient for cooking, at most 30 minutes, depending on the rice. A few minutes before serving mix a pinch of saffron with a little stock and stir in to give the risotto a delightful color. Add the remaining butter and serve with the grated Parmesan cheese in a separate dish. *Serves 4.*

RISOTTO WITH SHRIMP

½ cup butter	1½ cups Italian rice
2 onions, chopped	1¼ pints fish stock
1 clove garlic, crushed	pinch of saffron
salt and pepper	8 ounces large shrimp, shelled
4 tablespoons white wine	Parmesan cheese

Heat 6 tablespoons butter in a heavy pan and lightly fry the onion. Add half the garlic and the seasoning and simmer for a few minutes. Add wine and rice and cook for 10 minutes more. Add fish stock and a pinch of saffron, cover, and simmer over low heat until the rice is cooked and dry. While this is simmering, sauté the shrimp in the remaining butter and garlic. When done, combine with the rice and serve hot, with grated Parmesan cheese on the side.

Note: If you can obtain them, use Italian scampi instead of the shrimp. *Serves 4.*

Shellfish Risottos

Note: Many variations of the above may be made by substituting crab, lobster, scallops, etc. for the shrimp.

CRAB RISOTTO

1 clove garlic, chopped	1 large crab, cooked (or
6 tablespoons olive oil	equivalent amount canned
2 large tomatoes, peeled	crab meat)
3 ounces butter	salt and pepper
1½ cups rice	chopped parsley
2 pints stock	

Chop the garlic and brown it in oil, add the peeled tomatoes, and cook for 5 minutes. Keep warm. Melt the butter in a heavy saucepan; as it begins to brown, add the rice, mix well, and as that begins to brown, add the stock gradually and cook for 18 minutes or until the liquid is absorbed. Keeping the claw meat of the crab intact, if possible, chop the remainder of the crab meat and mix well with the rice. Adjust seasoning. Turn out onto a heated serving dish, lay the crab claw meat, cut into 4 pieces, on top, sprinkle with parsley and stand in the oven long enough for the crab meat to be heated through. *Serves 4.*

RISOTTO WITH MUSSELS

30 mussels
4 tablespoons olive oil
2 cloves garlic, crushed
2 large tomatoes, peeled
salt and pepper

2 tablespoons chopped parsley
¼ cup butter
1½ cups rice
1¼ cups fish stock

Scrub and beard the mussels thoroughly and wash under running water. Put a little oil in the bottom of a heavy pan and heat; add the mussels and cook for 5 minutes over fairly high heat so that the mussels will open and be cooked. Remove the mussels from their shells and set aside; discard the shells, but strain the liquor from the mussels into the stock and set aside. Cook the garlic and tomatoes for 10 minutes in a little oil, sufficient to make a sauce. Season with salt and pepper, remove from heat, and stir in the mussels and chopped parsley. Melt the butter and add the rice, stir well, then add the stock little by little and cook over a brisk heat for 18 minutes. Mix in the mussels and their sauce, adding a little more olive oil if necessary. *Serves 4.*

RISOTTO WITH FISH

½ cup butter	1 stalk celery, chopped
1 medium onion, sliced	1 tablespoon chopped parsley
1 pound white fish (filleted	1½ cups Italian rice
and cut into 1-inch squares)	3 pints fish stock
1 clove garlic, chopped	salt and pepper
1 carrot, sliced	grated Parmesan

Melt 6 tablespoons butter in a heavy saucepan and fry the onion, fish, and garlic until the onion and fish are slightly browned; add carrot, celery, and parsley and cook for 5 minutes more. Add the rice and cook for 15 minutes, stirring frequently, over moderate heat. Now add 2½ pints of stock (keeping ½ pint in reserve in case it is needed) and cover the saucepan tightly. Simmer over very low heat until the rice has absorbed the liquid and is cooked almost dry. Mix in remaining butter, adjust seasoning, and serve with grated Parmesan on the side. *Serves 4.*

MUSHROOM RISOTTO

Use the recipe for Risotto Milanese, but leave out the saffron and, instead of bone marrow, add ½ pound chopped mushrooms to the pan after browning the onion.

MUSHROOM AND CHICKEN-LIVER RISOTTO

2 onions, chopped	4 tablespoons white wine
¼ pound mushrooms, sliced	1 clove garlic, crushed
¼ pound chicken livers,	2 pints chicken stock
chopped	salt and pepper
½ cup butter	grated Parmesan
1½ cups Italian rice	

Fry onions, mushrooms, and chicken livers gently in ¼ cup butter in a heavy saucepan for about 5 minutes; add rice, wine, and garlic and cook for 15 minutes. Add stock and seasoning and simmer gently for 20 minutes, or until rice is tender and almost dry. Add remaining butter and serve with grated Parmesan cheese in a separate dish.   *Serves 4.*

CHICKEN RISOTTO

2 *pounds frying chicken pieces*
6 *tablespoons butter*
1 *medium-sized onion, sliced*
1½ *cups Italian rice*
4 *ounces cooked ham, diced*
1 *green pepper, seeded and sliced*
2 *large tomatoes, seeded and sliced*
1 *stalk celery, chopped*
¼ *pound mushrooms, sliced*
1 *clove garlic, crushed*
1 *glass white wine*
salt and pepper
pinch dried thyme
pinch dried basil
grated Parmesan

Put chicken pieces into 1½ pints water with a little salt, bring to boil, and simmer for 20 minutes. Remove from liquid and skin and bone the chicken, returning skin and bones to the pot and continue to simmer for stock. Dice the chicken fairly coarsely; heat 4 tablespoons butter in a deep pan, brown the onion, and add rice, ham, chicken, and vegetables. Fry gently for about 3 minutes. Add garlic and wine and simmer for a few minutes. Strain chicken stock into the pot, adding a little water if necessary to cover the contents. Season with salt, pepper, and herbs and bring to a boil, then simmer gently for about 20 minutes or until rice is tender and almost dry. Add remaining butter and serve with grated Parmesan on the side.   *Serves 4.*

ASPARAGUS RISOTTO

1 pound fresh asparagus (or
 equivalent canned)
¼ cup butter
1 small onion, chopped
1½ cups rice
2 pints stock

3 eggs
½ cup cream
4 tablespoons grated Parmesan
grated nutmeg
salt and pepper

If fresh asparagus is used, place in boiling water with a little salt until the asparagus is almost cooked. Use only the tips. If canned asparagus is used, no cooking is needed. Melt a little butter in a pan and cook the onion until translucent, add the rice, stir in well, and then add the stock little by little. Simmer gently until the rice is cooked. Put the rice into an ovenproof casserole, add a little butter, then lay the asparagus tips on top of the rice. Beat up the eggs with the cream, 2 tablespoons of grated Parmesan, a pinch of freshly grated nutmeg, and salt and pepper to taste. Pour the cream mixture over the asparagus and rice, sprinkle on another 2 tablespoons of Parmesan, and brown in a hot oven or under the grill. *Serves 4.*

RISI E BISI

This is a delightful Italian dish, which, history records, the doges of Venice used to favor; at any rate it has been well known in that part of Italy for centuries and is still highly popular.

2 tablespoons vegetable oil
¼ cup butter
4 ounces ham, diced
1 onion, chopped
2 stalks celery, chopped

3 cups shelled fresh peas
1½ cups rice
2½ pints stock
chopped parsley
grated Parmesan

Put the oil and half the butter into a heavy stock pan; cook the ham, onion, and celery for a few minutes. Add the peas and cook for 4 minutes more; then add the rice and about three quarters of the stock. Bring to a boil, reduce heat, and simmer gently until the rice and peas are cooked, about 30 minutes. Regulate the consistency of the soup by adding more stock if needed; the dish may be cooked longer until it is almost dry and used as a side dish for meat, etc., or served as soup with a garnish of chopped parsley and grated Parmesan cheese. *Serves 4.*

ITALIAN STUFFED PEPPERS (*Peperoni Ripieni*)

4 medium-sized green peppers
1 clove garlic, crushed
1⅓ cups fresh bread crumbs
2 tablespoons vegetable oil
1 2-ounce can anchovy fillets

4 tomatoes, chopped
2 tablespoons chopped parsley
¼ cup Italian long-grain rice
tomato sauce

Cut off the tops of the peppers; core, seed, and blanch them (including the tops) for 3 to 4 minutes in boiling water. Put the garlic and bread crumbs into very hot oil and fry for a few minutes. Chop the anchovy fillets and mix with the tomatoes, parsley, and rice; simmer until the tomatoes are soft. Place the peppers in a buttered ovenproof dish and fill with the rice mixture. Pour the remaining oil from the anchovies over the peppers and bake in a moderate oven (350° F.) for 20 minutes. Serve with a tomato sauce. *Serves 4.*

ITALIAN KIDNEYS AND RICE

2 calves' kidneys	*chopped parsley*
1 tablespoon flour	*5 ounces dry marsala wine*
6 tablespoons olive oil	*1 small onion, chopped*
6 tablespoons butter	*1½ cups rice*
1 clove garlic, chopped	*2 pints stock*
salt and pepper	

Trim the kidneys, soak them in cold water for 1 hour, wash again, then cut into small pieces. Flour the kidneys, heat a little of the oil and butter, cook kidneys with chopped garlic, season with salt and pepper and chopped parsley, and add the marsala. Cook briefly, then set aside; keep warm.

Heat remaining oil and butter in a heavy saucepan; brown the onion, which should be chopped very finely. Add the rice, mix well, then add the stock gradually and bring to a boil. Reduce heat and cook for 17 minutes. Put rice into a ring mold, set in a hot oven (450° F.) for a few minutes, and then turn out onto a heated serving dish. Serve with the kidneys in the center of the rice ring, garnished with a little parsley. *Serves 4.*

PICCATA WITH SAFFRON RICE

Piccata are very small escalopes of veal fried in a seasoned light egg batter. They are very well suited to saffron-colored rice.

1 pint chicken stock	Batter:
good pinch saffron	*2 eggs, separated*
1 cup rice	*4 tablespoons milk*
2 tablespoons butter	*2 tablespoons flour*
1 pound veal fillet	*pinch of salt*
vegetable oil or butter	*pepper*
2 lemons for garnish	*pinch of monosodium glutamate (optional)*

Put chicken stock into a pan with some salt and the saffron, bring to a boil, and add rice. Stir, bring to a boil again, reduce heat, and cover the pan tightly. Simmer gently for 20 minutes without opening the lid. Add butter, fork gently, and set aside. Keep warm.

Make a frying batter with the ingredients named: beat egg whites until stiff peaks form; beat the egg yolks and milk together, sift in the flour and seasonings, and fold in the egg whites. Cut the veal into very thin slices, about a dozen from the pound of veal. Incidentally, for the purpose of piccata you may sometimes find braising veal sufficiently good for your purpose (and considerably cheaper), depending on the way the butcher has cut it. Dip each piece of veal separately into the batter and fry in hot oil or butter, remembering that veal as thin as this will be cooked as soon as the batter is golden. Put the rice on a heated serving dish with the piccata ranged on top and garnished with sliced or quartered lemon. *Serves 4.*

Rice with the French

It ought to be said unequivocally from the start that the French are not a nation of rice eaters on the whole, although they do have some good rice dishes. They like to use rice in salads and some appetizers and a few soups; the best-known French main-course dish with rice is *Poule au Riz à la Crème* or Chicken with Rice and Cream Sauce. This is an excellent way of dealing with an elderly boiling fowl, which, of course, will have a very good flavor. More use is made of rice in France for desserts.

CHICKEN WITH RICE AND CREAM SAUCE
(*Poule au Riz à la Crème*)

6 ounces green bacon slices
butter
salt and pepper
1 teaspoon dried tarragon
juice of 1 lemon
1 boiling fowl, 4 to 5 pounds,
    dressed and trussed
4 onions, sliced
3 large carrots, sliced

5 pints chicken or veal stock
3 cloves garlic, crushed
1 bouquet garni
chopped parsley
2 cups medium-grain rice
2½ tablespoons flour
1¼ cups cream
2 egg yolks

Ideal for this dish is a fireproof and ovenproof pan with two small handles and a lid, which can be used on top of the stove or in the oven. Put the bacon slices (use regular bacon if you cannot get green) in the bottom of the pan with a little butter and fry gently. Season the bird inside with salt, pepper, and a little dried tarragon and 2 tablespoons butter, and rub the outside with lemon juice. Place chicken in the pot and brown slightly all over, adding sliced onion and carrot so that these can also brown in the bottom of the pan. Pour in boiling stock so that the bird is almost but not quite covered; season, add garlic, bouquet garni, and parsley. Cover the pan with foil and its lid and cook in a moderate oven (350° F.) for 2½ hours without lifting the lid. Now remove chicken carefully from the pot and, if necessary, add enough stock or water to make a total of 5 cups. Remove stock and set aside.

Boil rice for 10 minutes in plenty of salted boiling water, drain, and rinse. Put rice in the pot in which chicken was cooked, add 3¾ cups of the stock already set aside, and bring to a boil. Cover with foil and lid, then return it to the 350° F. oven for 30 minutes, by which time the rice should be almost dry and separated. Return the chicken to the pot on the rice or put the rice on a heated serving dish around the chicken; in any case keep warm.

Make a sauce by mixing 2½ tablespoons flour with 2½ table-spoons melted butter to form a roux. Then add remaining 1¼ cups of hot stock, stirring to obtain a smooth sauce. Stir in the cream; beat the 2 egg yolks and stir them into the cream sauce. Cook gently for 3 minutes without bringing to a boil, stir in chopped parsley, and serve with chicken and rice.   *Serves 4 to 6.*

PARISIAN CRAB AND RICE SALAD

This was a favorite summer dish in a small restaurant near the Sorbonne in Paris.

2 cups long-grain rice	*2 red peppers (canned or fresh)*
½ pound green beans	*1 cup vinaigrette made with*
1½ cups very young green	*mustard*
peas	*½ pound crab meat (fresh or*
salt	*canned)*
sugar	*3 hard-boiled eggs*
1 small bunch celery	*⅔ cup black olives*

The rice is cooked, in a large saucepan, by bringing 2½ pints of water, with 2 teaspoons of salt, to a boil and throwing the rice into it. When it comes to a boil again, lower the heat until it is just simmering and put the lid on the saucepan. Let it simmer for 15 minutes, then try a grain of the rice to make sure it is cooked, giving it another few minutes if necessary. Drain the rice, rinse it well in cold water, drain again, and dry it by putting it into a clean tea towel. Put it into the refrigerator.

Cut the beans into ½-inch lengths and lightly cook them in boiling water; do not overcook, for they must be firm. Do not cook the peas, but simply blanch them for 1 to 2 minutes in boiling water containing salt and sugar. Clean and cut the celery into inch-long pieces and finely dice the red peppers, keeping them in their oil or liquid if they are canned ones. Soak all the ingredients except the rice, crab, olives, and eggs in the vinaigrette; just before serving, mix in the rice and crab and garnish with slices of hard-boiled egg and the black olives. *Serves 6.*

ANNAMITE RICE

This makes an excellent accompaniment for fish or meat dishes that have a sauce with them.

1 cup rice	*salt*
5 pints water	*¼ cup butter*

Rinse the rice carefully in a colander under running water, then put it into the water, which should be boiling and salted with a teaspoon of salt, for 10 minutes. Drain and wash the rice, then dry. Put the rice into a saucepan that is only just big enough to hold it when it has finished swelling; add the butter in small pats and cook over a very slow heat for another 20 minutes, stirring once or twice with a fork to stop the rice from sticking. *Serves 4.*

SPICED RICE

An excellent accompaniment for fish or meat dishes.

1 cup long-grain rice	*1¼ cups water*
1 onion	*1 teaspoon paprika or curry or*
½ cup butter	*1 good pinch saffron*
salt	

Wash the rice in running water several times, drain; chop the onion finely. Heat the butter in a pan, then add the onion and rice and brown. Salt the water and bring to a boil, then add to the rice and onion. Bring to a boil, cover, and simmer over low heat for 15 minutes. By this time all the water should have been absorbed. Add whichever spice you have chosen and mix in well, giving the spice time to be absorbed before serving.   *Serves 4.*

RICE AND FISH RING

2 cups long-grain rice
¼ cup plus 1 teaspoon butter
2 tablespoons flour
2 teaspoons paprika
1¼ pints milk
16 ounces of canned pink
  salmon or tuna

good pinch saffron
2 teaspoons caraway seed
salt and pepper
chopped parsley

Wash the rice and put it into boiling salted water and simmer for 20 minutes. Drain, rinse, and keep hot. While rice is cooking, make a sauce with the ¼ cup butter, flour, paprika, and milk. Break up the fish and add it to the sauce. When this is heated through, remove from heat but keep warm. Mix saffron, caraway seed, extra teaspoon butter, and seasoning to taste into the rice until it is a uniform color. Then press the rice into a ring mold. Turn out onto a heated serving dish; with a slotted spoon put the pieces of fish into the center of the rice ring and pour the sauce over, leaving parts of the saffron-colored rice exposed so as to contrast with the rich paprika color of the sauce. Garnish with chopped parsley.   *Serves 5 to 6.*

SOUBISE RICE SAUCE

The normal soubise sauce is made with onion and a béchamel sauce. Rice helps to give it extra body and make it more of a garnish.

4 slices bacon	*¼ teaspoon sugar*
2 pounds onion, minced	*salt*
½ cup medium-grain rice	*¼ cup heavy cream*
1¼ cups chicken stock	*¼ cup butter*

Lay the bacon in the bottom of a saucepan and heat gently until the bottom of the pan is greased. Add the onions, washed rice, stock, ¼ teaspoon sugar, and salt to taste. Cook on very low heat until rice and onions are cooked, then press through a sieve or blend in blender; work in cream and butter and reheat without boiling. *Serves 4.*

TOMATO AND RICE SALAD *(Salade de Tomate au Riz)*

1½ cups rice	*grated nutmeg*
salt	*4 large tomatoes*
olive oil	*freshly ground black pepper*
tarragon vinegar	

Cook the rice as for Parisian Crab and Rice Salad (see page 82), but after drying it, mix in enough olive oil to cover each grain, then a little tarragon vinegar (just enough, so that it is not sloppy). Divide the rice on to 4 small dishes and grate a little nutmeg over it. Blanch and peel the tomatoes and slice each one thinly, setting these slices into the rice on each dish. Give each dish a good grinding of black pepper, after covering the tomatoes with a little mixed oil and vinegar. Put in the refrigerator and serve cold. *Serves 4.*

BASQUE MUSSELS AND RICE

You could call this French or Spanish, since the Basques claim some of each country. We were served it in a restaurant near the border, but in France.

2½ pints mussels, scraped and scrubbed clean
2½ pints fish stock
olive oil
1½ cups rice
1 small green pepper, sliced

4 ounces chorizo or similar garlic sausage, sliced
Spanish paprika
shrimp (optional)
lemon slices (optional)

First make sure the mussels are sound (not opened) and clean. Put them in a pan with some fish stock and a little olive oil and cook until they open, which takes only a few minutes. Leave them in their shells, remove from liquor, and keep warm. Put the rice in plenty of water, boil for about 7 to 8 minutes, then rinse in cold water and drain. Put it into a fireproof casserole or fairly deep dish, add the sliced pepper and sausage and a teaspoon of Spanish paprika, then strain onto this 2 pints of the liquor in which the mussels were cooked. Cover with tight lid or foil and simmer in a moderate oven (350° F.) for 25 minutes. Arrange mussels (left in their shells) on a heated serving dish and spread the rice around them. There should be just enough oily liquid in the rice to spoon a very small quantity over each mussel and so improve the appearance. If desired, the dish may be garnished with other seafood like shrimps and with lemon slices.   *Serves 4.*

CAMARGUE STEW AND RICE

If you travel down through the Camargue region of France to the west of Marseilles, where rice is now a successfully established crop, you are likely to find this stew served with saffron rice on the side.

vegetable oil	*salt and pepper*
¼ *pound green bacon, diced*	*5 ounces red wine*
1 carrot, sliced	*1 bouquet garni*
1 large tomato, sliced	*a little stock*
1 large onion, sliced	*1½ cups rice*
2 cloves garlic, crushed	*1 good pinch saffron*
1½ pounds good stewing beef,	*chopped parsley*
cut into 1-inch cubes	

Heat some oil in the bottom of a heavy pan and gently fry the bacon (use regular bacon if green is unobtainable), carrot, tomato, onion, and garlic for 5 minutes; add the beef, and cook for 10 minutes more. Season. Add wine (after reducing it by one third in another pan), bouquet garni, and a little stock, bring to a boil, reduce heat, cover the pan tightly, and simmer very gently (or cook in very slow oven) for 2½ hours. While the stew is cooking, boil rice in salted water, with the saffron, drain, and rinse well; keep warm. Add a little chopped parsley to the stew, cook for 5 minutes more, and serve with rice on the side. *Serves 4.*

RIZ À L'IMPÉRATRICE

This French dessert is one of the great classic dishes of all time, a rather unlikely one, in fact, when it is remembered that the French are not particularly rice-minded and that it took a long time to introduce this food into France. Many variations are possible, using the original dish for the centerpiece.

½ cup short-grain rice
1½ pints milk
vanilla extract
2 tablespoons butter
½ cup sugar
¾ cup candied fruits
  (cherry, pineapple, etc.),
  chopped

3 tablespoons kirsch
4 egg yolks
unflavored gelatine
1¼ cups heavy cream
red currant jelly (or similar)

Rinse the rice, dry, then put it into 1 pint of milk with a few drops of vanilla extract and bring to a boil. Reduce heat and simmer gently until the rice is cooked and the milk absorbed. Add the butter and ¼ cup sugar and mix well. Steep the chopped candied fruit in the kirsch for several hours. Make a custard by creaming the egg yolks with the remaining sugar, and boiling the remaining milk and pouring it over the eggs and sugar. Into this custard stir about ½ ounce (½ envelope) of gelatine (already softened in water) and keep stirring until the gelatine is quite incorporated. Mix this in with the now-cold rice.

Sprinkle the candied fruits and kirsch over the top of this mixture. Whip the cream (not too stiffly) and spread over the top of the whole dish, then fold in so that the cream and the candied fruits are well incorporated in the whole. Turn the mixture into a lightly greased charlotte (or similar) mold and put it in the refrigerator to set. When serving, turn out onto a dish and surround with a little red currant jelly diluted with water. (You could use apricot or other preserves or jelly instead.)   *Serves 4.*

PEARS, PEACHES, STRAWBERRIES, APRICOTS, ETC., À L'IMPÉRATRICE

Use the previous recipe to make a centerpiece but eliminate the red currant (or other) sauce. Instead, set the rice mold in the center of a larger dish and surround it with cooked pears, peaches, strawberries, apricots, or whatever you choose, in a decorative way and with a little of the fruit in the center of the mold, if it is of the ring type.

Rice with the Spaniards and Portuguese

I cannot imagine Spanish food without liberal amounts of rice any more than I can imagine the bull ring in Barcelona without bull-fights, or the nightclubs of the popular resorts without their flamenco dancers, or the broad *ramblas* without their leafy shade in summer and the drowsy buzz of the siesta hour when everyone except mad Englishmen are having their afternoon rest. Spain grows some of her own rice, but only an eighth, say, of what comes out of India; and so more has to be imported, particularly to satisfy the maw of about 20 million tourists who come every year, as much for the colorful food as for the sunshine and beaches.

The Spanish national dish, you might say, is paella. Of course, it varies from place to place, the coastal resorts combining fish, meat, poultry, and rice in a very special way and some of the inland towns, where fish is not a practical proposition, concentrating more on meat. The Mediterranean coast produces what I think is the best example of this dish.

Manuel Garzaran—Manolo to the thousands who visit him every year—opened up a restaurant on the beach at Torredembarra, a resort village eight miles north of the onetime Spanish capital Tarragona, in the days before almost the whole of the Spanish coastline had been turned into a concrete canyon of apartment blocks. It was called Al Gusto, and no matter how other ventures fared, Manolo and his wife, Carmen, always had a full restaurant and I believe that paella, as he cooked it, was the reason. People always go where the food is good. Manolo recently sold the Al Gusto and built another place called the Xaica. The paella remained of the same high quality, so what better way of demonstrating the paella of the Mediterranean coast, the Paella Valenciana, than to quote his recipe for it.

PAELLA VALENCIANA—XAICA RECIPE
(*Torredembarra*)

1 medium-sized chicken, cut into about 12 or more pieces
vegetable oil
salt
1½ cups green peas
¾ cup lima beans
½ pound pork fillet, cut into small squares
8 ounces calamar or squid, cut into small pieces
1 cup chopped onions
4 cloves garlic, crushed
1 red pepper, cut into squares
¾ pound tomatoes, peeled and chopped
8 ounces chorizo sausage, sliced
3 cups rice
6 ounces shelled large shrimp
6 jumbo shrimp (in shells)
24 mussels
good pinch of saffron

Fry the chicken pieces in a little oil and some salt in a large saucepan. Boil the peas and beans in salted water. When the chicken is almost cooked, add the pieces of pork and calamar, put the lid on the pan, and cook over low heat for 5 minutes; add the onions, garlic, and red pepper and cook for a few minutes, then the tomatoes and sausage and then, a few moments later, the rice. After a few minutes' cooking the mixture may now be transferred to a paella pan (or a large, shallow fireproof dish) and mixed with a fork to ensure that the contents are equally divided among six portions. Mix in the lima beans and peas evenly; then divide the shelled shrimp and the jumbo shrimp and mussels (their shells scrubbed and washed) over the top. Put a pinch of saffron into 1½ cups of boiling water and pour this gently into the paella dish so as not to disturb the contents. Bring to a boil and simmer gently for 15 to 20 minutes, by which time the rice should be almost dry. This may be done in the oven. Let the paella rest in a cool oven for another 5 minutes before serving. *Serves 6.*

BASQUE PAELLA

Here is a paella we found when traveling back through the Basque country from Spain. It is milder than the heavier varieties of the south but still has the unmistakable tang of Spanish cooking.

olive oil

¼ *pound thick green bacon, diced*

1 *small rabbit, jointed into 8 pieces*

1½ *cups rice*

1 *pound filleted white fish (cod, halibut, etc.), cut up*

1½ *cups peas (cooked)*

1 *large onion, chopped*

4 *ounces chorizo or similar small garlic sausage, sliced*

2 *cloves garlic, chopped*

20 *mussels*

6 *ounces shelled shrimp*

4 *jumbo shrimp, cooked in shells*

1 *red pepper and 1 green pepper*

⅔ *cup green olives, stoned*

⅔ *cup black olives, stoned*

good pinch saffron

2 *pints chicken stock*

salt and pepper

Note that olive oil is used, making the dish softer than if a harsher oil were employed. Heat it in a heavy pan, brown the bacon (use regular bacon if you cannot get green) and the rabbit, then add the rice and fry it until the rice loses its darker color and turns white. It should be well stirred during this time.

Now arrange the whole dish as you wish it to appear when

finished, in a large shallow ovenproof dish. There should be equal amounts of all ingredients in each quarter of the dish. Mussels should be well cleaned and low enough to be almost covered by the saffron-colored stock when it is poured carefully over the whole. Peppers should be chopped to 1-inch triangles and, with the shrimp and olives, placed on top of the dish for the maximum effect. The whole is then covered with a lid (if there is one) or foil and baked in a moderate oven (350° F.) for 25 minutes. The dish that was served to us had little extras like *cipirones,* which are not easily obtainable here, and a special type of Basque sausage like chorizo. *Serves 4.*

COUNTRY PAELLA (*Paella Campina*)

Traditionally paella in Spain implies fish, chicken, and meat mixed in the rice dish. But there are many areas where fish is not obtainable because of the vast distances in Spain and methods of transporting frozen foods that would put the fish beyond the reach of many country people. Here, then, is a typical country paella, made without the fish.

1 *small chicken, jointed into*	*vegetable oil*
8 pieces	*1½ cups rice*
½ *pound of boiling bacon,*	*3 cloves garlic, chopped*
cut into inch cubes	*cloves*
4 ounces chorizo or garlic	*bay leaf*
sausage, sliced	*2 pints chicken or veal stock*
bits of rabbit, game birds, etc.	*salt and pepper*
(optional)	

Fry chicken, bacon, and any other uncooked meats until brown and half cooked in a little good vegetable oil. Put all the other ingredients in with the meat and the oil in which it was cooked and bring to a boil, cover, and simmer either on top of the stove or in a moderate oven (350° F.) until the meats are fully cooked, the rice tender, and the liquid absorbed. Keep a little stock handy in case the paella dries before the food is cooked and tender. *Serves 4.*

VEGETABLE PAELLA

You will probably not find this sort of peasant's paella (or vegetarian's) along the built-up tourist belt, but it is often made in poorer areas and certainly deserves a better fate than being labeled "poor man's food."

vegetable oil	*1½ cups rice*
2 cloves garlic, crushed	*pinch saffron*
selection of vegetables, such	*salt and pepper*
as trimmed green artichokes,	*2½ pints stock*
zucchini, eggplants, sliced red	
peppers, etc.	

Heat some oil in a large pan with crushed garlic cloves and lightly fry the vegetables. Drain vegetables and set aside, then add rice to the oil and stir until each grain is covered with a film of oil. Add saffron, seasoning, and 2 pints of stock, bring to a boil, and simmer for 25 minutes until rice is almost dry. Shortly before serving add the vegetables to the rice and stir lightly. Add more stock if necessary. *Serves 4.*

PAELLA WITH MEMORIES OF MAJORCA

Everyone who goes for a Spanish vacation comes back with happy memories—and a recipe for paella. Rex and Peggy Elliott are two such people, and frequently Rex takes over the kitchen on a Saturday night and makes the Surrey, England, version of the Majorca paella. Here is his recipe—lighthearted, but then, as he says, it's a lighthearted dish, and if you're not in that mood cook something else.

1 *LP record of nostalgic*
   Spanish vacation music
1 *bottle of red Rioja wine*
   (mostly for the cook)
12 *mussels*
2 *chicken leg quarters,*
   cooked
1 *red pepper*
1 *green pepper*
4 *tomatoes*
4 *ounces lean pork fillet*

1 *tablespoon olive oil*
2 *cloves garlic, peeled and*
   chopped
4 *teacups long-grain rice*
pinch of saffron (or substitute)
1¼ *pints chicken stock*
4 *ounces cooked and shelled*
   shrimp
1 *cup frozen peas*
12 *whole jumbo shrimp,*
   cooked unshelled

You need a warm kitchen. Put on the LP record, take a glass of the wine, and start: scrape the mussels with a knife, scrub and remove the beard, wash thoroughly under running water. Break the chicken legs away from the rest of the quarters, remove the skin, and slice the skin into strips. Cut the ends off the peppers and slice these into thin strips. Remove core and seeds from remainder of the peppers, and slice them. Quarter the tomatoes and remove the seeds. Cut the pork into ¾-inch cubes.

Turn over the record, take another glass of wine, and start cooking: put the oil, garlic, chicken skin slices, and the sliced pepper ends into a 12-inch paella dish, or frying pan (preferably non-stick) and fry gently for 4 to 5 minutes. Do not let the chicken skin go crisp. Add pork and continue frying gently until the pork is cooked. Stir well; do not let the pork brown too much. Then push the contents of the pan to the sides and let the oil seep back to the center. Put the rice in the center and, when it is covered with oil, mix all the contents thoroughly. Do not let the rice burn. At this stage it might not look wonderful but it smells delicious. Stir the saffron into the stock, add to the pan, and bring to a boil. Add the chicken pieces, tomatoes, peppers, mussels, and shelled shrimp. Bring to a boil again and reduce heat to a simmer. Stir for a minute or two to ensure a good mix, cover the pan with foil, and simmer for 20 minutes. Recount vacation tales with your guests. Remove foil and add peas, stir, put foil on the pan again, and simmer for 15 minutes more.

Assuming you have not drunk too much of the wine, you should be left by now with only the unshelled jumbo shrimp. Put these in a circle around the dish, half buried in the rice, replace foil, and simmer for another 10 minutes, or until the liquid as such has been absorbed but the rice is still moist without being soggy. Finish off under hot broiler for 1 to 2 minutes, until shrimp shells begin to show white patches.   *Serves 4.*

SPANISH RICE AND VERMICELLI
VEGETABLE SOUP   (*Sopa Mezclada*)

3 *potatoes (new if possible)*	*soaked and boiled until*
2 *medium-sized white turnips*	*tender*
½ *small white cabbage,*	1 *clove garlic*
shredded	3 *ounces rice*
2 *large carrots, thick-sliced*	*good pinch of saffron*
4 *stalks celery, rough-chopped*	3 *ounces vermicelli*
3¾ *pints good veal stock*	*salt and pepper*
⅔ *cup dried haricot beans,*	

Prepare the vegetables. Bring the stock to a boil in a large stock-pot and, when boiling, add the haricot beans, the potatoes, turnips, cabbage, carrots, celery, and garlic. Bring to a boil again, then reduce the heat and simmer very gently for several hours with the lid firmly on the pot. Half an hour before cooking is completed, add the rice, the saffron dissolved in a tablespoon of warm water, then the vermicelli and whatever salt and pepper seasoning is needed. Since the soup will be really thick, serve it in winter. *Serves 4.*

XAICA SEAFOOD RICE (*Arroz a la Marinera Xaica*)

There are many ways of cooking seafood with rice. This is one that Manuel Garzaran uses in his Xaica restaurant at Torredembarra. If angler fish is not available, any firm white fish will do as a substitute.

vegetable oil	*¾ pound tomatoes (fresh or*
18 mussels	*canned)*
6 clams (fresh or canned)	*2½ cups rice*
2 cloves garlic, chopped	*12 ounces angler fish, cut up*
1¾ cups chopped onion	*8 ounces large shrimp, shelled*
8 ounces squid (or canned	*salt and pepper*
calamar)	*1½ cups green peas*
8 ounces cuttlefish	*1 red pepper, cut in strips*

Heat some oil in a big saucepan and add the mussels and clams, all well scrubbed. When they have cooked sufficiently to open them, remove the shells. Now add the garlic and onion, well chopped, to the mussels and clams in the pan and cook for a few minutes. Chop the calamar and cuttlefish into small pieces and add these and the tomatoes and cook for 10 minutes. Add the rice and cook for a few minutes, making sure the rice is covered with a film of oil. Add 1½ cups boiling water, the pieces of angler fish, and the shrimp, neatly arranged. Season with salt (and pepper if desired) and add the green peas and strips of red pepper. Bring to a boil and simmer for 20 minutes, then leave for 5 minutes to settle before serving.   *Serves 6.*

CHICKEN WITH RICE: 1 (*Arroz con Pollo: I*)

This is one of the classic dishes of Spain, one that is still served almost everywhere you go in both the tourist parts and the purely Spanish parts of the country. There are many recipes, but here are the three you are most likely to find and the easiest adapted to American cooking.

1 chicken, about 3 or 4 pounds, jointed	*1 bay leaf*
	1 teaspoon oregano powder
salt and pepper	*good pinch saffron*
good pinch paprika	*2 pints chicken stock*
vegetable oil	*1½ cups rice*
1 large onion, chopped	*2¼ cups green peas*
2 cloves garlic, chopped	*3 red peppers, blanched, cored,*
16-ounce can tomatoes	*and seeded*

Season the chicken with salt, pepper, and a dusting of paprika. Heat oil in a deep frying pan and brown chicken joints all over, remove, and place in a roasting pan that has a top cover to it. Brown onion and garlic in the same oil that the chicken was browned in, then add the tomatoes (complete with liquid from the can), bay leaf, oregano, saffron, and salt and pepper if required, pour in the stock, and bring to a boil. Pour over and around the chicken and add the rice, then cover with the lid and put into a preheated moderate oven (350° F.) for 25 minutes, or until rice is cooked and tender. While it is cooking, cook the peas and cut the peppers into strips. Fork the rice a little, stir in the peas and red peppers, and return to oven, without lid, for about 10 minutes. *Serves 4.*

CHICKEN WITH RICE: 2   (*Arroz con Pollo: 2*)

vegetable oil
2 onions, chopped
1 clove garlic, crushed
4 ounces bacon
2 medium-sized tomatoes,
*   peeled*
salt and pepper
2 small roasting chickens,
*   jointed*

1½ cups rice
2½ pints chicken stock
1 green pepper, sliced
1 red pepper, sliced
1½ cups green peas
chopped parsley

Heat a little oil in a large pan with a lid, and fry the onion and garlic until the onion is translucent. Add the bacon, in small pieces, and tomato in slices. Fry briefly and remove the vegetables, then season the chicken joints and brown in the same oil. Return vegetables to the pan, add the rice, and stir well, then add the stock, cover, bring to a boil, reduce heat and simmer until the liquid is absorbed. While this is cooking, lightly fry the peppers and green peas. Serve the chicken nicely arranged on the rice, using the peppers, peas, and parsley as garnish.   *Serves 4.*

CHICKEN WITH RICE: 3   (*Arroz con Pollo: 3*)

2 very small chickens or
*   squabs, each quartered*
6 ounces ham, cubed
¼ cup butter
2 large onions, sliced
2 large tomatoes, quartered
1½ cups rice
2½ pints chicken stock

salt and pepper
2 red peppers, sliced
vegetable oil
1½ cups green peas, cooked
1 small can asparagus tips
*   (or fresh)*
chopped parsley

Fry the chicken quarters (they should be very, very small chickens) and ham together in butter until browned. Add onion and tomato and fry for a few minutes, then add rice and mix well. Add stock and seasoning, cover, and simmer until the rice is almost dry. Fry peppers lightly in a little oil, then add peas and asparagus only long enough to heat them. Serve the chicken and rice with the peppers, asparagus, and peas, as well as the chopped parsley, arranged around the serving dish. *Serves 4.*

SPANISH COD AND RICE

In the normal way in Spain, this dish would probably be made with salt cod, but in America the unsalted fish would be more suitable and, in fact, less trouble. This recipe is designed as an appetizer; for main course, increase fish quantity.

vegetable oil	*1 large onion, chopped*
12 ounces cod	*1½ cups rice*
1 clove garlic, crushed	*1¼ pints fish stock*
2 tomatoes, chopped	*salt and pepper*

Heat some oil in a heavy pan and lightly fry the cod, breaking it into 1-inch squares. Add garlic, tomatoes, and onion and fry for a few minutes, then add rice and mix so that all the rice is covered with a film of oil. Add stock, bring to a boil, reduce heat, and simmer until the rice has absorbed all the liquid. Season to taste. *Serves 4.*

SOUTHERN SPANISH FISH WITH RICE

1 *pound white fish fillets*	*pinch dried mixed herbs*
(reserve head and bones)	*salt and pepper*
1 *small glass white wine*	*vegetable oil*
1 *onion*	2 *cloves garlic, crushed*
1 *carrot*	1½ *cups rice*
1 *stalk celery*	2 *tomatoes, seeded and chopped*

Make a fumet with the head and bones of the fish, the wine, onion, carrot, celery, and herbs, salt and pepper, plus sufficient water. Put the oil in a pan with garlic and heat, fry fish until cooked and browned, remove fish, cool, and break into 1-inch-square pieces. Put rice into a paella dish (or roasting dish) with the oil and garlic from cooking the fish, plus about 1¼ pints of the stock, and cook over fairly high heat until the rice is tender and the stock absorbed. Arrange fish and tomato over the rice and dry off in oven a few minutes before serving.   *Serves 4.*

SPANISH KIDNEYS AND RICE   (*Riñones a lo Español*)

1½ *cups rice*	*salt and freshly ground black*
pinch saffron	*pepper*
vegetable oil	8 *lambs' kidneys*
1 *glass dry sherry*	*flour*
1 *clove garlic, crushed*	

Cook the rice in water with a pinch of saffron to color it, until rice is almost dry. Make a marinade of 2 tablespoons oil, the sherry, garlic, and salt and black pepper, halve the kidneys and marinate them in this briefly, thread onto 4 skewers and broil, basting with the marinade. Add a little flour to the marinade in a pan and cook until thick (add water if too thick), and use as a sauce to pour over the kidneys, which should be served on a bed of rice still on their skewers. *Serves 4.*

GALICIAN RICE *(Arroz con Leche a lo Gallego)*

1 cup short-grain rice
1 cup sugar
salt
6 tablespoons butter

ground nutmeg (or flavoring
  to choice)
2½ pints milk

An excellent rice dessert dish. In this case the rice is washed under running water for a short time before being put into boiling water. The water is brought to a boil again and kept at the boiling point for about 5 minutes, then the rice is washed in cold running water in a sieve. Add most of the sugar, good pinch of salt, butter, and flavoring to the milk and bring it to a boil; add the rice, bring to a boil again, reduce heat, and simmer gently for 30 minutes with the lid of the pan tightly closed. By this time the rice should be almost dry. Remove, place in a frying pan with enough butter to grease the bottom, dry for a few minutes, sprinkle with remaining sugar, and finish off under the broiler, when the surface should be a nice golden brown. In Galicia, of course, this used to be finished off under a red-hot salamander. *Serves 4.*

ZAMORA PORK AND RICE

This is something of a novelty from Old Castile and you are not seriously expected to cook it. But if you have a pork butcher who is willing to supply the necessary parts of the pig, and you have the patience, here is how it is done.

4 ounces pork fat
6 onions, sliced
2 turnips, sliced
2 cloves garlic, crushed
1 teaspoon paprika
1 bouquet garni
salt and pepper
¾ pound chopped pork or
    smoked ham

2 pig's trotters (scalded,
    boned, and diced)
1 pig's chap, boned and
    chopped
1 pig's ear, boned and
    chopped
2½ pints boiling stock
1 cup rice
6 slices bacon

Heat the fat and part-cook the onions and turnips, then add the herbs and seasoning, the pork meat except the bacon, and about 2 pints boiling stock and simmer gently for about 3 hours. Add more stock if necessary. Add the rice, boil for 15 minutes, stirring all the time. Now lay the bacon on top of the contents of the pan and cook under a hot broiler until the bacon is cooked. *Serves 5 to 6.*

PORTUGUESE LOBSTER AND RICE

vegetable oil
2 cloves garlic, crushed
12 ounces lobster meat
1 small sole, filleted
4 tomatoes, peeled
2 red peppers
1 green pepper

1 cup rice
2 pints boiling stock (about)
1 pinch saffron
a few asparagus tips
1 cup green peas, cooked
salt and pepper

Heat some oil in a heavy pan, fry the garlic and lobster briefly, add sole, tomatoes, and peppers, cook briefly, add rice, 1½ pints stock, and the saffron and simmer for 25 minutes. Add more stock as necessary. Then add asparagus tips and green peas as garnish, leaving the dish over the heat only long enough to heat these through. Adjust seasoning. Serve hot. *Serves 4.*

ALGARVE COD AND RICE

The Portuguese are great fishermen and their boats fish the cod banks, returning with fine catches of fresh cod, which is preferred to the salted variety more normally used in the Mediterranean countries. Here is the sort of *bacalhau fresco* or fresh cod dish you will find there.

¼ *cup butter*
3 *onions, chopped*
2 *cloves garlic, crushed*
5 *ounces vegetable oil*
5 *cod steaks, about 6 to 8*
   ounces each
9 *ounces rice*

5 *large tomatoes (or 1*
   16-ounce can tomatoes)
5 *ounces dry white wine*
salt and pepper
chopped parsley
sliced lemon

Heat the butter in a sauté pan (the type with a lid) and fry the onions and garlic until slightly colored; add the oil, heat, and cook the fish in this until a golden color. While this is being done, boil the rice in salted water for 10 minutes, rinse, and drain well. Add the rice, tomatoes (peeled and chopped), the wine, and the seasoning to the pan and cook over medium heat with the lid tightly closed for about 10 minutes. Add the chopped parsley, cook for another 10 minutes, and then serve the fish covered with the rice and tomato mixture from the pan. Top each cod steak with a couple of lemon slices. *Serves 5.*

Rice with the Russians

In a country as big as the Soviet Union, whose staple diet until recently has been rye bread, it is not surprising that rice does not play a very great part in the nation's diet. But in some parts, particularly the Caucasus, bordering the area where rice is the basic food, and in other places adjoining great rice-eating countries, there is quite a large consumption of rice.

In the old days when the aristocracy dined on caviar, sturgeon, trout, lobster, beef with sour cream, and the like, they also had rice in one or another luxurious form; the peasants, if they ate it at all, would have had it plain and boiled, at best perhaps with a little *smetana*, or sour cream, on it. Nowadays more rice recipes are in use in the country, some of which appear in the following pages.

KOULIBIAC WITH SALMON AND RICE

Russians love these dishes, which are baked with choux pastry and various fillings, not unlike a pie. Here is one with salmon, but ground meat, hard-boiled eggs, and various other fillings may be substituted.

½ *cup rice*	1 *piece fennel, chopped*
1 *pound choux pastry*	16 *ounces canned salmon*
1 *large onion, chopped*	*milk*
4 *ounces mushrooms, chopped*	1 *tablespoon butter*

Cook the rice, drain well, and allow to cool. Roll out the choux pastry into 2 large rectangular sheets. On one place a layer of cooked rice, some chopped onion, mushrooms, and fennel, then another layer of rice, a layer of salmon and the remaining onion, mushrooms, and fennel, and then another layer of rice. Then place the second sheet of choux pastry over the whole and seal the edges of the 2 sheets of pastry with a little milk. Leave a steam escape hole in the top of the koulibiac, brush it with melted butter, and put in a moderate oven (350° F.) and bake for about 45 minutes. The finished "pie" should be golden brown. *Serves 5 to 6.*

KARAVAI

This dish uses the Russian pancake, or blini, with bone marrow, currants, rice, and other ingredients.

Blini:
½ *ounce yeast (or equivalent in dried yeast)*
1¼ *pints milk*
2¼ *cups flour (buckwheat flour is traditional)*
2 *eggs (separated)*
salt
6 *tablespoons butter*

Karavai:
1¼ *cups rice*
8 *ounces beef marrow, poached and diced*
2 *tablespoons currants*
salt and pepper

Cook rice, drain, and dry. Make the blini by dissolving the yeast in about half the milk, which should be warmed, and making a dough with a small quantity of the flour. Let this rise for 2 hours, then mix in the egg yolks, a pinch of salt, and the rest of the milk. Beat the egg whites until stiff and fold into the mixture, let it stand for 30 minutes, and then fry the pancakes in butter in a pan so that they are thin and about the same diameter as whatever small round cake tin you have. Lay one blini on the bottom of the tin, spread with a layer of cooked rice, sprinkle over this the chopped marrow and some currants, with seasoning as desired, and then another blini over this. Repeat this until the materials have been used up (finishing with a blini on the top), cover with foil, and bake in a moderate oven (350° F.) for 30 minutes, then serve hot. *Serves 4.*

SHASHLIK WITH RICE

1 pound fillet of lamb, or lean meat cut from the leg	salt and pepper
	¼ pound bacon slices
vinegar	1½ cups rice
1 onion, chopped	eggplant (optional)
vegetable oil	cucumber (optional)

Cut the meat into 1-inch cubes and marinate for several hours in vinegar with a little water, the onion, ½ tablespoon oil, and salt and pepper.

Thread the lamb onto skewers with a square of bacon in between each cube. Boil the rice, drain, dry, and keep warm. When it is ready, broil the meat under a hot broiler or over a barbecue fire, basting with a little oil. If desired, pieces of eggplant or cucumber may be added to the skewers. Serve on a bed of hot rice. *Serves 4.*

CAUCASIAN PILAF

Shashlik is a Caucasian dish, but people of that region also like mutton cooked into a pilaf, as set out below. This is more suitable for older mutton.

vegetable oil	1 pint stock
1 onion, chopped	1½ cups rice
1½ pounds mutton (or lamb)	1 bay leaf
	a few peppercorns
salt and pepper	

Heat a little oil in a heavy pan and cook the onion until it begins to brown. Cut the meat into small slices, season with salt and pepper, and fry in the oil. When it begins to color, add the stock and cook for 20 minutes. Blanch the rice in boiling water for a few minutes, drain and dry, and add to the pot, with the bay leaf and peppercorns. Cover tightly and simmer gently until the rice is almost dry and quite cooked. *Serves 4.*

SMETANA CUCUMBERS

¼ cup rice
1 large or 2 smaller
  cucumbers
½ pound cooked meat,
  chopped

2 tablespoons butter
salt and pepper
1¼ cups sour cream

An excellent way of using up the end of the meat from Sunday dinner. Cook the rice, drain, and cool. Cut the cucumber into 4, halve these pieces lengthwise, and scoop out the seeds. Fry the rice and chopped meat in the butter with salt and pepper. When beginning to brown, fill the scooped-out cucumbers with the mixture, cover with sour cream, and bake in a moderate oven (350° F.) for about 20 minutes. *Serves 4.*

BEEF STROGANOFF WITH RICE

1 cup long-grain rice
1½ pounds fillet steak
salt and freshly ground
  black pepper
3 onions, sliced

¼ cup butter
4 ounces mushrooms, sliced
pinch of mustard
1¼ cups sour cream
flour (optional)

Boil the rice in salted water for 20 minutes, drain and rinse, keep hot. Cut the steak into strips about 2 inches long and as thick as your little finger; season with salt and freshly ground black pepper. Some cooks like to chill the meat before it is cooked, but this is optional. Fry the onions gently in some of the butter until they begin to color, drain, and set aside. Cook mushrooms in the same butter, drain, and put them with the onions, keeping them warm. Increase the heat and fry the steak so quickly that it is sealed on the outside and cooked inside before the blood and juices have a chance to run out of it. Put the meat, onions, and mushrooms back in the pan, adjust the seasoning, add a pinch of dry mustard and the remaining butter, then stir in the sour cream. Bring to a boil and serve immediately on a bed of rice. (If the mixture looks too thin, stir in a little flour before serving and cook for another couple of minutes.)   *Serves 4.*

Other European Rice

AUSTRIAN TRAUTMANSDORFF RICE

A classic dish in Austria, named after the Trautmansdorff family who were prominent in Austria in the seventeenth century, about the time of the Thirty Years War. It bears a certain resemblance to the French Riz à l'Impératrice.

¾ *cup short-grain rice*
1¼ *scant pints milk*
1 *vanilla pod (or extract)*
3 *ounces sugar*
pinch of salt

½ *ounce (½ envelope)*
    unflavored gelatine
2 *tablespoons maraschino*
1¼ *cups cream, whipped*
1 *cup candied fruit, diced*

Put the rice in a saucepan with all but 2 tablespoons of the milk, add the vanilla flavoring, sugar, and a pinch of salt, and bring to a boil. Put foil over the pan and then the lid, and simmer very gently until the rice has absorbed the milk. Set the rice aside to cool (remembering to remove the vanilla pod if one was used). Dissolve the gelatine in the remaining milk over low heat. Blend the maraschino into the whipped cream; mix the gelatine into the rice, then stir in the candied fruit, fold in the cream, spoon into a mold, and chill in the refrigerator. When ready to serve, turn out on to a serving dish, and garnish with a little more candied fruit or a sweet sauce. *Serves 4.*

YUGOSLAV DJUVECH

2 tomatoes	*¼ pint olive oil*
2 eggplants, peeled	*Spanish paprika powder*
¾ pound lamb	*5 ounces rice*
¾ pound lean pork	*6 ounces Gruyère cheese,*
1 clove garlic, chopped finely	*grated (about 1½ cups*
3 green peppers, cut into	*grated)*
½-inch squares	*chopped parsley*
salt and pepper	

Slice the tomatoes thinly, and the eggplants not quite so thin. Slice the meat about ¼ inch thick and put a layer of lamb and pork on the bottom of an ovenproof casserole. Put a layer of slices of tomato and eggplant over the meat, then a sprinkling of the chopped garlic and peppers over that. Sprinkle a little salt and pepper over, then a little olive oil, and a pinch of paprika. Repeat these layers until the ingredients are used up, put the lid on the casserole, and bake in a moderate oven (350° F.) until the meat is tender and cooked, about 1½ hours. When the casserole has been in the oven for an hour, boil the rice in salted water for 20 minutes, drain, rinse, and drain, keeping warm. When the casserole is cooked, spread rice over the top, then cover with the grated Gruyère and a little oil. Return to the oven until the rice is heated through and the cheese browned. Sprinkle another pinch of paprika and give the dish a garnish of parsley. *Serves 4 to 5.*

YUGOSLAV SARMA

This is a sort of Yugoslav dolmas, which can be made with either cabbage or vine leaves.

2½ ounces rice	chopped parsley
8 cabbage (or vine) leaves	1 egg
6 tablespoons butter	salt and pepper
1 clove garlic, crushed	1¼ cups chicken stock
2 onions, chopped	6 tablespoons fresh bread
¾ pound ground meat	crumbs
5 ounces raisins	

Cook the rice in boiling salted water, drain well, and set aside. Drop the leaves into boiling salted water and cook until tender. Drain carefully and set aside. Heat 4 tablespoons butter in a pan and add garlic. Add onion and fry until translucent, then add ground meat and cook until the meat is browned. Mix in previously cooked rice and raisins, cook for 2 minutes, then set aside. When cool, add chopped parsley to taste and bind the mixture with beaten egg, after seasoning to taste with salt and pepper. Divide the mixture into 8 and put 1 portion on each leaf. Wrap the leaves so as to form rolls or square parcels, place them in an ovenproof casserole, and pour the stock over them. Cover and cook in a moderate oven (350° F.) until most of the liquid has disappeared, then sprinkle with the bread crumbs, dipped in the remaining melted butter, and brown under the broiler. *Serves 4.*

YUGOSLAV SATARAS

1½ cups rice	1 tablespoon paprika
½ pound each of beef, pork, and lamb, cut into 1-inch cubes	1 teaspoon ground cumin seed
	salt and pepper
	4 green peppers, chopped
6 tablespoons butter	3 tomatoes, chopped
3 onions, chopped	½ cup sour cream
1 clove garlic, crushed	

Cook the rice in boiling water, drain, and keep warm. Fry the meat in melted butter in a heavy pan, shaking the pan to make sure the pieces of meat are browned on all sides, then add onion, garlic, and paprika and fry for 5 minutes more. Add a little water and the cumin powder, season with salt and pepper to taste, and simmer gently with the lid on for ¾ hour. Add green pepper and chopped tomato, replace lid, and simmer again until cooked. Blend in the cream away from the heat, return to the stove for a minute or two to reheat, but do not boil. Serve with rice in a separate bowl.   *Serves 4 to 5.*

RICE OPEN SANDWICHES

1 cup rice	1 tablespoon chopped parsley
3 tablespoons butter	salt and pepper
1 egg, beaten	

Boil the rice in salted water until tender, drain; while still hot add the butter, mix well, then stir in egg, parsley, and seasoning to taste. Spread over the bottom of a large, shallow baking tin and put into a preheated moderate oven (375° F.) and bake for 10 minutes. Cool and cut into pieces the size required for use in Danish open sandwiches, to take the place of bread.

Toppings can be the same as for the ordinary open sandwiches.

American Rice Dishes

Not only has the United States become one of the world's largest rice-growing countries, but Americans have found a vast new food horizon in cooking it. In a country where publicists really lay on the pressure when they set out to make a product known and popular, the people who are responsible for keeping the word "rice" before the public have collected a magnificent array of recipes for today's tastes. Some of these dishes are extremely good; and as befits a nation in a hurry, many are geared to use with canned, frozen, or other convenience foods. I shall try here to give a number of representative recipes that use a minimum of convenience foods.

AMERICAN SHRIMP AND RICE

½ cup butter
1¼ cups rice
1 large onion, finely chopped
4 ounces mushrooms, sliced
1 green pepper, chopped
good pinch nutmeg
salt and black pepper

1 cup dry white wine
1½ pints chicken stock
2 tablespoons chopped parsley
1 bay leaf
¼ teaspoon dried thyme
12 ounces large shrimp, shelled

Heat the butter in a heavy saucepan and cook the rice, onions, mushrooms, green pepper, nutmeg, and seasoning until the rice turns a golden color. Add the wine and cook for a few minutes, then add the stock and herbs, cover, and simmer for 15 minutes. Add the shrimp and, if they are already cooked, leave in the pot only long enough to heat up. If they are not cooked, simmer for 15 minutes more before serving. *Serves 4.*

PORK CHOPS AND MUSHROOM RICE

4 pork chops
shortening
1 cup rice
1 onion, finely chopped

1 package mushroom soup mix
½ cup sour cream
salt and pepper

Fry the pork chops in shortening, turning them so that they are browned on both sides and tender. Remove chops from the pan; keep warm. Add rice and onion to the pan and fry until the onion is tender. Replace chops in the pan with the onions and rice. Mix mushroom soup with water according to instructions on package, stir in the sour cream, and pour over the chops. Adjust seasoning. Bring almost to a boil, then reduce heat and simmer with lid on the pan for 20 minutes.   *Serves 4.*

QUAIL WITH RICE

6 ounces Madeira wine
3 tablespoons seedless raisins
2 cloves
½ cup rice
½ teaspoon grated orange peel
¼ teaspoon ground ginger

¼ cup pecans, chopped
6 tablespoons butter
juice of ½ orange
4 quail
salt and black pepper
4 ounces brandy

Pour the wine into a saucepan, add the raisins and cloves, and bring to a boil; reduce heat, simmer for a few minutes, then strain. Set aside the liquor and pick cloves out of raisins and discard the cloves. Mix the raisins with the rice, orange peel, ground ginger, chopped pecans, and about 1 tablespoon of butter. Wipe over the quail with a damp clean cloth and stuff them with the butter and nut mixture.

Melt the remaining butter in a roasting pan, add the Madeira wine that was set aside and the orange juice, mix well; place a wire rack in the pan, put the quail on it, baste them with some of the Madeira mixture in the pan, then put it into a preheated oven (450° F.) for a few minutes. Reduce the oven to slow (300° F.) and bake for 25 minutes, basting 3 times with the mixture in the pan. Now place the quail in a heated metal serving dish (or fireproof china or glass one) and heat over a spirit lamp. Reduce the gravy in the pan, season, and pour over the quail. Then heat the brandy, ignite it, and pour over the quail. Serve as soon as the flame dies out.   *Serves 4.*

FRANKS AND CALICO RICE

1½ cups rice
1½ pints chicken stock
3 tablespoons olive oil
1½ tablespoons vinegar
1½ tablespoons mustard
salt and pepper
2 hard-boiled eggs, chopped
⅔ cup green olives, sliced
4 stalks celery, finely diced

2 large onions, chopped
4 tablespoons mixed pickles, chopped
4 slices Canadian bacon (fried crisp and then crumbled)
1½ pounds frankfurters, cooked
⅓ cup black olives

Cook rice in the chicken stock, drain, and keep hot. While it is cooking blend the oil, vinegar, mustard, and salt and pepper to taste. Pour this over the hot rice and mix well. Add the hard-boiled eggs, green olives, celery, onion, pickles, and bacon and mix well. Cut the frankfurters to half their length and stand them on the cut ends in a circular ovenproof casserole dish. Fill the dish with the rice mixture and top with black olives. Put into a preheated hot oven (450° F.) and bake for 15 minutes.   *Serves 6 to 8.*

SUKIYAKI

Strictly speaking, Sukiyaki is a Japanese dish, but there is a big Japanese-American population on the West Coast, and this is how they make it.

1½ pounds lean beef, cubed
1 tablespoon vegetable oil
1 large onion
6 small carrots
2 stalks celery
1 pound green beans, sliced
4 large scallions

2 green peppers
4 leaves Chinese cabbage,
    sliced
soy sauce
1 tablespoon sugar
1½ cups rice, cooked

Brown the meat in the oil. Cut the vegetables diagonally into small pieces and arrange over the meat, with onions first, then the carrots, celery, green beans, scallions, green pepper, and Chinese cabbage. Cover tightly and cook over steam until the vegetables are half cooked, then add soy sauce (to taste) and sugar. Resume cooking until the vegetables are tender, but they must not be mushy. Serve on a bed of hot cooked rice, with additional soy sauce separate. *Serves 6.*

AMERICAN CURRIED CHICKEN AND RICE

1½ cups rice
1 large onion, chopped
1 clove garlic, chopped
2 stalks celery, chopped
½ teaspoon mustard
1 large cooking apple, peeled
    and diced
4 ounces thick bacon, diced
½ cup butter

2 teaspoons curry powder
1 ounce flour
½ teaspoon ground mace
1 bouquet garni
1¼ pints stock
salt and pepper
meat from medium-sized
    roasting chicken, raw, cubed

Cook the rice, drain, and keep warm. Fry the onion, garlic, celery, mustard, apple, and bacon in butter gently for 10 minutes. Add the curry powder, flour, and ground mace and cook for 5 minutes more, then press through a sieve. Return the strained liquid to the pot, add the bouquet garni, stock, and seasoning if necessary, bring to a boil, and then simmer gently, covered, for 30 minutes. Add the chicken and simmer again for 30 minutes (or less if chicken is cooked). Serve on a bed of hot rice. *Serves 4.*

ROAST VEAL BREAST WITH LEMON RICE STUFFING

¾ cup rice
3 ounces seedless raisins
1 teaspoon grated lemon peel
2 tablespoons chopped parsley
½ teaspoon basil
1 clove garlic, chopped
  (optional)

salt and pepper
1 5-pound breast of veal
4 strips larding pork or fat
  bacon slices
2 tablespoons shortening

Ask the butcher to see that the veal has a pocket ready for stuffing.
    Cook the rice, drain, and dry. Mix the rice, raisins, lemon peel, parsley, basil, and garlic (if used). Season and stuff the pocket of the veal with the mixture. Secure with skewers or string. Lay larding pork (or bacon) on top of the roast and place it on the shortening in a roasting pan. Put into a preheated moderately slow oven (325° F.) and cook for 2½ hours, or until meat is tender. *Serves 6.*

CHICKEN À LA KING

1½ cups rice
3¾ cups chicken stock
1 green pepper, chopped
2 stalks celery, chopped
2 small onions, chopped
3 tablespoons flour
5 ounces dry white wine

3 tablespoons heavy cream
1 small roasting chicken,
   cooked, boned, and diced
1 red pepper, cut into strips
1 bouquet garni
salt and pepper

Cook the rice in boiling chicken stock. Drain and dry the rice, return the stock to the pot, add the green pepper, celery, and onion and simmer until the vegetables are tender. Mix the flour and wine together and stir into the broth, slowly add the cream, and stir until thick (do not boil after the cream has been added). Add the chicken, red pepper strips, and seasonings and when heated through, serve on a bed of the rice, or with rice on the side. *Serves 4.*

RICE PUFFIN RING WITH EGGS

½ cup rice
4 eggs
milk
½ cup strong cheese, grated

1 cup unsifted flour
1 teaspoon salt
1½ teaspoons baking powder
1 tablespoon chopped parsley

Cook rice in boiling salted water, drain and dry. Whisk 2 eggs until frothy, stir in rice, ½ cup milk, grated cheese; sift into the mixture the flour, salt, and baking powder. Stir well until thoroughly blended. Line a ring mold with greased paper (or well grease the mold itself) and fill the mold with the mixture. Put into a preheated moderately hot oven (425° F.) and bake for 30 minutes. Just before it is cooked, scramble the remaining eggs with a little milk and chopped parsley. Turn out the rice ring and serve with the scrambled eggs in the center.   *Serves 2.*

HOT GERMAN SALAD

1 cup rice
12 ounce frankfurters, cut
into ½-inch lengths
4 large stalks celery, diced
1 large onion, chopped
½ cup mayonnaise
1½ tablespoons flour

2 teaspoons mustard, mixed
with little water
salt and pepper
½ cup milk
garnish of sliced hard-boiled
egg and parsley sprigs

Boil the rice, drain, and keep warm. Mix in with it the pieces of frankfurter, celery, and onion, place in a casserole and pour over it a mixture made by blending the mayonnaise, flour, mustard, seasoning, and milk. Cover with foil and put into a preheated moderate oven (350° F.) for 30 minutes. Garnish with the slices of egg and sprigs of parsley.   *Serves 4.*

AMERICAN RICE SALAD

1½ cups rice
2 pints chicken stock
2 medium-sized green and 1
large red pepper, chopped
4 large stalks celery, chopped
1 large onion, chopped

4 tablespoons prepared oil
and vinegar dressing
salt and pepper
4 tomatoes, sliced and
quartered

Cook the rice in the chicken broth until tender, almost dry, and fluffy. Combine it with the peppers, celery, onion, and enough dressing to cover each grain of rice but without being sloppy. Season to taste. Turn out on to a salad dish and surround with tomatoes. *Serves 4.*

LOUISIANA RICE

1½ cups rice
2 pints stock
salt and pepper
2 onions, sliced

2 tablespoons butter
1 medium-sized red pepper, chopped

Cook the rice in the stock until almost dry and fluffy; season. Sauté the onion in the butter; when golden brown add the rice and red pepper and cook until the rice is heated through, stirring occasionally. *Serves 4.*

CHICKEN VERMOUTH WITH RICE

1 frying chicken, about 3 pounds, jointed into 8 pieces
salt and pepper
½ cup dry white vermouth
3 carrots, sliced
2 stalks celery, sliced
1 large onion, sliced thinly

4 cloves garlic, peeled but not crushed
2 tablespoons chopped parsley
1 cup long-grain rice
stock for cooking rice (optional)
3 tablespoons sour cream

Put the chicken into a casserole, preferably one with a tight-fitting lid, season with salt and pepper, add the vermouth, carrots, celery, onion, garlic, and parsley, cover with a double thickness of baking foil and then the lid, and bake in a preheated moderately hot oven (375° F.) for 1½ hours, without lifting the cover. While the chicken is cooking, cook the rice in 1¼ pints of stock, or water if no stock is available, and have it warm and fluffy when the chicken is ready to serve. Stir sour cream into the gravy of the chicken and serve on a bed of rice. (If you dislike garlic, leave it out, but some people take three times as much as the amount indicated above.)   *Serves 4.*

GINGER LAMB WITH RICE

4 ounces ginger snaps, finely
  crushed
1 pound ground lamb
1 teaspoon garlic salt
salt and pepper
1 egg, beaten
1 8-ounce can pineapple slices
1 large green pepper, seeded
  and cut into 1-inch squares

2 tablespoons brown sugar
1 teaspoon dry mustard
juice of 1 lemon
¼ teaspoon ground ginger
tomato ketchup
1½ cups long-grain rice,
  cooked

The cookies must be fresh: crush them between sheets of waxed paper or in a clean dish towel, or in a clean electric coffee grinder. Mix them with the lamb, garlic salt, some salt and pepper, and beaten egg and, when thoroughly blended, make into balls about 1½ inches in diameter. Cut the pineapple slices into 4 and thread skewers alternately with meat balls, pineapple, meat balls, green pepper, meat balls, etc. Make a thickish mixture of the sugar, mustard, lemon juice, ground ginger, and tomato ketchup and brush the skewers well with this. Cook under a hot broiler for about 8 minutes, turning several times and basting with more sauce mixture when they begin to dry out. Serve on a bed of previously cooked fluffy rice. *Serves 4.*

TEXAS BEEF HASH

8 ounces ground beef
1 large green and 1 large red
   pepper, diced
2 tablespoons butter

1 cup rice
1 pint beef stock
salt and pepper

Fry the beef and peppers in butter until the peppers are tender. Add rice, stock, and seasoning and bring to a boil. Stir, cover, reduce heat, and simmer for 20 minutes, or until the rice is almost dry and tender. Serve hot.   *Serves 4.*

TEXAS CHICKEN HASH

As for Texas Beef Hash, but use chicken instead of beef, and chicken stock instead of beef stock.

QUICK CHICKEN CASSEROLE

This dish can be prepared almost in a jiffy from canned soups and already cooked chicken. Almost in a jiffy?—well, at a great saving of trouble and only about half an hour for cooking.

1 10-ounce can cream of
   mushroom soup
1 10-ounce can cream of
   chicken soup
chicken stock
1½ cups rice
1 teaspoon onion powder or
   essence

1 chicken, 3 to 4 pounds,
   cooked and boned
½ red pepper, chopped
1 cup grated Cheddar cheese
   (or Gruyère)

Put the 2 cans of soup in a casserole with an amount of stock equal to ½ of one of the soup cans. Heat and mix well. Add all the other ingredients except cheese. Put the lid on the casserole dish and cook in a moderately hot oven (375° F.) for 30 minutes. Sprinkle with grated cheese.   *Serves 6 to 8.*

HAMBURGER AND TOMATO PARMESAN RICE

2 tablespoons butter
1 large onion, chopped
1 clove garlic, crushed
1½ cups rice

1 10-ounce can tomato soup
salt and pepper
¼ cup grated Parmesan cheese
4 large hamburgers

Heat the butter in a heavy pan, fry onion and garlic until the onion is tender, then add rice and cook until golden, stirring constantly. Add tomato soup and a generous 1¼ cups of water, season with salt and pepper, bring to a boil, cover, and simmer gently for 25 minutes, until rice is tender and the liquid absorbed. Remove from stove, stir in Parmesan. Fry or broil hamburgers or cook them on the griddle, and serve on a bed of the hot rice.   *Serves 4.*

RICE FOR ROAST BEEF

This recipe for rice is an accompaniment for roast beef. One might serve another vegetable as well.

2 tablespoons butter
1 clove garlic, crushed
2 tablespoons flour
1 teaspoon paprika

1¼ cups milk
salt and pepper
1 cup rice
1 cup grated Gruyère cheese

Melt butter in small pan, add garlic, cook for 2 minutes, stir in flour, and mix well. Add paprika, milk, salt and pepper to taste. Put the rice in a buttered ovenproof dish, pour mixture over, and top with grated cheese. Cover and bake at moderate heat (350° F.) in the oven for 30 minutes, then uncover and bake for 5 minutes more. *Serves 4.*

GOLDEN RICE BEEFBURGER PIE

2 cups rice	1 tablespoon hot barbecue
2 pints beef stock	sauce
1¼ cups onion, chopped	4 ounces sliced mushrooms
4 stalks celery, chopped	salt and pepper
1 large green pepper, chopped	2 tablespoons very finely
2 tablespoons butter	chopped parsley
1 pound extra-lean ground	1 small red pepper, chopped
beef	1 tablespoon mustard, mixed
8 tablespoons tomato	in water
ketchup	2 eggs, beaten

Cook the rice in the beef stock for about 25 minutes over a low heat, until the rice is tender and the liquid absorbed.

Fry the onions, celery, and green pepper gently in butter without browning. Remove from the heat and mix in the ground meat, sauces, mushrooms, and salt and pepper. Place mixture in a fairly deep round baking dish.

Mix the rice with the chopped parsley, red pepper, mustard, salt and pepper, and the 2 beaten eggs and spread over the top of the mixture in the baking dish, leaving a small circular part at the center uncovered. Cover with lid or foil and bake in a preheated moderately hot oven (400° F.) for 30 minutes. Serve hot. *Serves 6.*

NEW JERSEY RICE AND TOMATO

¼ cup butter
1 cup rice
1 large onion, chopped
1 clove garlic, crushed
1 small green pepper,
  chopped

1 16-ounce can tomato juice
1½ cups grated cheese
16 stuffed olives
salt and pepper

Heat the butter and lightly fry the rice, onion, garlic, and green pepper until the onion is lightly browned. Add three quarters of the tomato juice and a scant 1¼ cups of boiling water. Bring to a boil, reduce heat, and simmer gently until the liquid is absorbed and the rice fluffy. Mix a small amount of the cheese and the olives into the rice, adjust seasoning, place in a casserole dish, pour the rest of the tomato juice over the mixture and top with rest of the grated cheese. Put into a moderately hot preheated oven (400° F.) until the dish is brown on top and heated through. *Serves 4.*

JAMBALAYAS

You cannot ignore Creole cookery, the lovely dishes for which recipes have been handed down among the top families of New Orleans from the days when proud French colonists called it *la Nouvelle Orléans* and, even though born there, were more French than the French themselves. They refused to change their ways even when the land became subject to the Spanish throne, and both they and the Spanish inhabitants kept their own ways of life when the place was sold to America under the Louisiana Purchase. Even today Creole cookery is a thing apart, not only from the cuisine of the United States but even from French, Spanish, and other cuisines. It owes much to the extraordinary finesse that black female cooks, most of West African origin, were able to bring to the original French or Spanish recipes.

Since it is rice-growing country and since much of the culinary heritage was Spanish, it is not surprising that there are many rice dishes. The jambalayas are among the best known, and for them there are countless recipes. They have the advantage of being dishes that can be cooked for the most part a day or two before needed, and simply finished off in the oven for 45 minutes on the night. Here are some typical jambalaya recipes.

JAMBALAYA WITH CHICKEN AND HAM

¼ cup butter
2 large onions, finely chopped
2 cloves garlic, crushed
2 green peppers, finely chopped
½ pound cooked chicken,
    diced
½ pound cooked ham, diced
12 Vienna sausages, each cut
    into 3

1½ cups rice
1 16-ounce can tomatoes
1¼ pints chicken stock
1 tablespoon chopped parsley
½ teaspoon dried thyme
¼ teaspoon hot chili powder
salt and freshly ground black
    pepper

Heat the butter in a heavy pan, fry the onion, garlic, and green pepper until the onion is tender; stir, add chicken, ham, and sausages, and cook for 6 minutes. Put the mixture into a large casserole, adding the rice, the tomatoes and their liquid, the stock (using a little to wash out the pan and add this to the casserole), and all the seasonings. Cover tightly (with foil and a lid) and put into a preheated moderate oven (350° F.) and cook for 1½ or 1¾ hours.   *Serves 6.*

JAMBALAYA WITH PORK AND PEAS

1⅓ *cups dried peas*	1 *large onion, chopped*
1½ *cups rice*	½ *teaspoon hot chili powder*
12 *ounces salt pork*	*salt and pepper* (*if needed*)

Soak the peas overnight. Bring a large pan of salted water to a boil and add the rice, keeping it at a fast boil for 15 minutes. Remove, drain, and wash the rice in cold water, drain, and dry. Put the drained peas into a saucepan, cover with water, bring to a boil and add the pork, chopped into half-finger-size pieces, and the chopped onion. Simmer gently until the meat is tender and most of the water evaporated. Add the chili powder, stir, then add the rice and keep on a low heat only long enough to heat the rice, which should be well stirred in. Adjust seasoning if necessary. *Serves 4.*

My favorite jambalayas are those made with fish, preferably shellfish, the lovely big shrimp or tasty crabs from that part of the world. The following recipe is for shrimp, but a wide variety of variations is possible with different seafoods.

SHRIMP JAMBALAYA

1½ *cups rice*	½ *red pepper, chopped*
1 *large onion*	½ *teaspoon chili powder*
1 *clove garlic, crushed*	(*or cayenne pepper*)
¼ *cup butter*	*salt and pepper*
8 *ounces tomatoes* (*fresh or*	8 *ounces cooked and shelled*
canned)	*large shrimp*

Cook rice as for Jambalaya with Pork and Peas. Drain and dry.

Fry the onion and garlic in a heavy pan in butter until brown, add the tomatoes (chopped if you are using fresh ones), the red pepper and seasonings, then the shelled shrimp, and simmer gently for about 15 minutes. If you use uncooked fish, longer cooking time will be necessary.   *Serves 4.*

GUMBOS

The gumbos are another very distinctive feature of Creole cookery, and some devotees of this sort of dish insist that nowhere else in the world but New Orleans, once a historic outpost of French colonialism, will you find them cooked as well. Be that as it may, the dishes are quite peculiar to this part of the world and owe their distinctive taste either to the vegetable called okra, or lady's finger, or to the powdered dried leaves of the sassafras tree, called *filé*, which the early settlers learned about from the Choctaw Indians. There are a great many recipes for various gumbo dishes; here are a few worth trying. Okra may be purchased in most good food markets and *filé* in specialty stores. As originally made, the gumbos were very rich dishes, but the less-rich forms are still very attractive.

CHICKEN GUMBO FILÉ

The rice in this dish is an accompaniment and should be cooked to coincide with completion of the cooking of the soup.

1 boiling fowl
½ pound ham
3 ounces butter
½ red chili pepper, seeded and chopped
2 onions, chopped
salt and cayenne pepper

1 bouquet garni
5 pints chicken stock
¾ cup rice
2 dozen oysters (fresh or canned—optional)
2 tablespoons filé *powder*

Joint the fowl into 8 pieces; cut the ham into ½-inch dice. Melt the butter in a heavy, large stockpot and add the chicken and ham, shaking the pot until they have browned all over. Add the chili pepper and onion and cook for another few minutes, until the onion is brown. Add seasoning, bouquet garni, and 4 pints of stock (including the oyster liquor, if used). Bring to a boil, then reduce heat, cover tightly with lid, and simmer gently for 2 hours. Add more stock if required. Meanwhile, boil, drain, and keep rice warm. Ten minutes before serving, take the chicken from the pot, remove some of the meat, and return this meat to the pot, leaving the rest of the chicken for other purposes. Reheat and after 5 minutes add the oysters, if used, and stir in the *filé* powder. Reheat, without boiling, and serve with the rice.   *Serves 6 to 8.*

CHICKEN OKRA GUMBO

As with the Gumbo *Filé*, the rice in this dish is cooked to coincide with the end of the cooking of the soup and is served with it.

1 boiling fowl	1 pound okra, sliced
1 pound ham	1 bouquet garni
3 ounces butter	salt and cayenne pepper
½ hot red chili pepper, seeded and chopped	5 pints chicken stock
2 onions, chopped	¾ cup rice
4 tomatoes, peeled and chopped	

Joint the fowl into 8 pieces; dice the ham. Heat the butter in a heavy stockpot and add the chicken and ham, shaking the pot until they have browned all over. Add the chili pepper and the onion and cook again until the onion is brown. Add the tomatoes and simmer for 2 or 3 minutes; then add the okra, simmering until the okra turns brown. Add the bouquet garni, seasoning, and 4 pints of chicken stock, leaving 1 pint in reserve in case it is needed during cooking. Bring to a boil, reduce heat, cover tightly, and simmer gently 2 hours. Meantime, boil, drain, and keep rice warm. Serve hot, with pieces of the chicken, which will have left the carcass by then, included in each serving, and boiled rice on the side. *Serves 6 to 8.*

SHELLFISH GUMBO

¾ cup rice
4 ounces ham, diced
¼ cup butter
1 large onion, chopped
1 pound okra (sliced)
4 good-sized tomatoes (fresh or canned)
1 clove garlic, crushed
½ lemon, sliced thinly

1 bouquet garni
2½ pints fish stock
¼ teaspoon Tabasco sauce
1 teaspoon Worcestershire sauce
salt and paprika
2 tablespoons flour
1 8-ounce can crab meat (or 2 small crabs)

Cook the rice while the gumbo is cooking, timing its completion to coincide with that of the dish. Fry the diced ham gently in a minimal amount of butter, add the onion, and cook until brown, then add the okra, tomatoes, garlic, and lemon, as well as the bouquet garni and 2 pints of fish stock, which for preference should be made with the shellfish being used. Bring to a boil and add the two sauces, salt to taste, and about ¼ teaspoon paprika. Cover, reduce heat, and simmer gently for 1½ hours. Thicken the pot with a roux made of the flour and the remaining butter, cook until smooth, stirring continually, then add the crab meat. (If canned crab is used it will not need cooking. If fresh crabs are used they must be cooked and the meat removed from the shell before being put into the gumbo.) Serve very hot, with hot rice. *Serves 4.*

The same recipe may be used for shrimp, lobster, scallops, and other shellfish, but cook them all before adding them to the gumbo.

OLD-FASHIONED RICE PUDDING

3 ounces seeded raisins   salt
¼ cup rice   1 teaspoon vanilla extract
3¾ cups milk   grated nutmeg
½ cup sugar

Soak the raisins in water. Put the rice, milk, sugar, and salt to taste in an ovenproof baking dish and bake in a preheated slow oven (300° F.) for 2 hours. Add the raisins, vanilla extract, and two good pinches of grated nutmeg and return to the oven for ½ hour. *Serves 6.*

CHERRIES IN THE SNOW

1 cup short-grain rice   Sauce:
1½ pints milk   1 16-ounce can pitted sour
½ cup sugar   cherries
2 tablespoons butter   ¾ cup sugar
1 envelope (1 tablespoon)   2 tablespoons arrowroot or
   unflavored gelatine   cornstarch
1 teaspoon almond extract   red food coloring (optional)
½ cup heavy cream,
   whipped

Cook the rice, drain, and allow to cool. Mix the rice, 1¼ pints of the milk, the sugar, and the butter and cook over low heat, stirring until the mixture has thickened. Soften the gelatine in the remaining milk, standing the bowl of milk in hot water to dissolve the gelatine. Stir this into the rice mixture with the almond extract, then cool. Fold the whipped cream into this mixture and turn into 8 or 9 (or 10 if possible) individual molds, or one large mold.

Serve it with a sauce made as follows: drain the syrup from the cherries and set the cherries aside. Mix the sugar and arrowroot into the juice, adding a drop or two of red food coloring if the cherry juice is not sufficiently red. Stir over low heat until the mixture thickens. Replace the cherries and let the sauce cool. *Serves 8 to 10.*

EGG, BRANDY, AND RICE PIE

¼ cup short-grain rice
1¼ cups milk
3 eggs, separated
½ cup sugar
pinch of nutmeg
pinch of salt
1 envelope (1 tablespoon)
*   unflavored gelatine*

3 tablespoons sweet sherry
2 tablespoons brandy
5 ounces heavy cream

Crumb Crust:
¾ pound sweet chocolate
*   cookies*
6 tablespoons butter, melted

Cook the rice, drain, and set aside. Bring the milk almost to a boil in the top of a double boiler; mix the egg yolks, half the sugar, a pinch of nutmeg, and a small pinch of salt and stir gently into the milk. Cook, stirring constantly, until thick enough to coat a spoon. Soften the gelatine in 2 tablespoons of water, dissolve in the custard. Mix in the rice and cook until creamy. Add the sherry and brandy, stir in well, and allow the mixture to cool. Make the crumb crust: crush the cookies to fine crumbs between two clean cloths with a rolling pin and mix with the melted butter. Press the mixture into the sides and bottom of a 9-inch pie plate and put it into a preheated moderately hot oven (400° F.)

for 10 minutes, and allow to cool. Turn filling into the crumb crust and chill. Whip remaining sugar with the cream and serve the whole with whipped cream on top.   *Serves 4.*

Latin American Rice

CHICKEN WITH RICE, MEXICAN STYLE
(*Arroz con Pollo a lo Mexicano*)

1 *medium-sized chicken,*	½ *cup dry white wine*
cut into 8 pieces	2 *pints stock*
¼ *cup butter*	2 *tomatoes, chopped*
2 *large onions, chopped*	½ *teaspoon hot chili pepper*
2 *cloves garlic, crushed*	1 *bouquet garni*
1 *large green pepper,*	1 *small red pepper, chopped*
chopped	*salt and pepper*
2 *stalks celery, chopped*	1½ *cups rice*
good pinch of saffron	*grated Parmesan cheese*

Sauté the chicken pieces slowly in butter but without browning them. Add onions, garlic, and green pepper, and cook for several minutes, then add the celery and saffron and simmer for 5 minutes, stirring the mixture well to work in the saffron. Add the wine, stock, tomatoes, chili pepper, bouquet garni, and red pepper, then season to taste. Simmer for 20 minutes with the lid on the pan, then add the rice, bring to a boil, cover tightly, and simmer gently (or put in a moderate oven [350° F.]) for 20 minutes, or until the rice is cooked. Serve hot, after removing bouquet garni, with Parmesan on the side.   *Serves 4.*

ARGENTINE CARBONNADE WITH RICE

1 pound beef or veal
1 tablespoon flour
salt
shortening
1 clove garlic, chopped
2 onions, chopped
2 green peppers, chopped
3 tomatoes, chopped
½ bunch celery (about 5
  stalks)
1 carrot, sliced
1 small white turnip, cut up
1 small leek, sliced
2 sprigs parsley
1 bay leaf
cayenne pepper

3 peppercorns
1 bouquet garni
1¼ pints beef stock
1¼ cups white wine
2 tart apples, peeled, cored,
  and chopped
4 medium-sized potatoes,
  quartered
½ pound pumpkin, peeled
  and cut up
2 peaches, cut up
¼ pound grapes, separated
4 ounces corn kernels,
  cooked
1½ cups long-grain rice,
  cooked

Cut the meat into pieces about 1½ inches, drop into a bag of flour and salt, coat well, fry in heated shortening in a big pan. When brown, take out the meat and fry the garlic, onions, green peppers, and tomatoes in the fat, then return the meat to the pot and add the celery, chopped into ¾-inch lengths. Add the pot vegetables and the seasonings, the beef stock, and the wine and simmer for 1 hour with the lid tightly on the pan. Add the apples, potatoes, and pumpkin and cook for 20 minutes more, until potatoes are cooked. Just before serving (in a decorative ovenproof bowl for preference), add the fruit and the corn and keep on the heat only long enough for these to be heated. Meantime, cook the rice, drain, and keep hot. It may be served in a side dish.   *Serves 5 to 6.*

CHILEAN ARROZ CON CONGRIO (*Conger Eel and Rice*)

1¼ cups rice
4 conger eel steaks (about
    1½ pounds altogether; or
    substitute other type of eel)
½ cup wine
a few peppercorns
salt and pepper
vegetable oil

¼ cup butter
4 onions, chopped
2 cloves garlic, crushed
½ teaspoon each dried cumin
    seed and marjoram
4 large tomatoes, peeled and
    sliced

Cook the rice for 10 minutes in boiling water; drain. Poach the eel gently for about 15 minutes in water and wine, with a few peppercorns. Drain. Reserve the liquor, later to be used as stock. Season the eel steaks with salt and pepper and cook in hot oil until brown. Heat the butter in a sauté pan with lid, fry the onion and garlic gently, stirring in the cumin and marjoram, then add the tomatoes and cook for 10 minutes. Add the partly cooked rice and the fish, with enough of the fish stock to cover, and cook with the lid on for about 30 minutes on low heat or in a slow oven, until the fish is quite cooked and the rice tender and most of the liquid absorbed. Conger eel—or any other type of eel —should always be well cooked, since it tends to be rather indigestible otherwise. *Serves 4.*

BRAZILIAN FEIJOADA

1 cup rice
1⅓ cups dried black beans
2 large onions, chopped
2 cloves garlic, crushed
vegetable oil
1 pound pork, diced
6 ounces chorizo sausage
1 green pepper, chopped

1 red pepper, cut in strips
4 tomatoes (or 1 16-ounce
    can)
pinch saffron
¾ teaspoon thyme
½ teaspoon marjoram
salt and pepper
1¼ cups stock

Boil the rice, drain, and set aside. Drain the beans, after soaking them overnight, put into fresh water, and let them simmer gently for several hours, until tender. Fry the onions and garlic lightly in oil, then add the pork and sausage and cook until brown. Add the peppers and cook for 5 minutes, then add the rice, beans, tomatoes, saffron, thyme, marjoram, and seasoning and stock and cook for 20 minutes more. Serve hot. *Serves 4.*

Rice in the British Commonwealth

"COLONIAL GOOSE" WITH RICE

There is a theory that Australians, who are not really overfond of their lamb as a food, try to disguise its origins wherever possible. This, then, is presumably one way of so doing.

1 cup rice	*salt and cayenne pepper*
2 lambs' kidneys	*1 leg or shoulder of lamb,*
4 slices bacon	*about 4 pounds, boned*
2 onions	*1 teaspoon mustard,*
2 tablespoons bread crumbs	*moistened*
1 egg	*1 tablespoon honey*

Boil the rice, drain well, and set aside. Blanch, trim, and skin the kidneys, then chop them finely. Chop bacon and finely chop the onions. Moisten the bread crumbs. Make a stuffing of all the ingredients except the lamb, mustard, and honey and fill the lamb. Tie it in such a way that it looks like the neck and body of a goose, which should be easy enough after a little practice. Bake in a moderate to moderately hot oven (375° F.) for 1 hour

20 minutes, then mix mustard and honey together and glaze the lamb with it before baking another 20 minutes. *Serves 6 (or more)*.

AUSTRALIAN CHICKEN AND RICE SALAD

1¼ cups rice
1½ pounds diced cooked
    chicken
4 large stalks celery, sliced
2 large oranges, peeled and
    broken into sections
1 tablespoon chopped chives

salt and pepper
½ cup sour cream
1 cup mayonnaise
½ small red pepper, chopped
    finely
⅓ cup chopped roasted
    almonds

Cook the rice in plenty of boiling salted water until tender, drain, and cool. Put the rice, chicken, celery, orange sections, chives, and salt and pepper into a salad bowl and toss well. Mix the sour cream and mayonnaise and pour over the salad, then mix it in well. Garnish with sprinklings of the red pepper and chopped almonds. *Serves 4*.

PINEAPPLE RICE RITZ

½ cup short-grain rice
1 pint milk
2 teaspoons grated orange
    peel
2 tablespoons butter
1 large can (about 29
    ounces) pineapple slices,
    drained
3 ounces candied cherries
1 tablespoon sherry

juice of 1 orange and 1
    lemon
3 tablespoons sugar
3 ounces chopped mixed peel
5 ounces cream, whipped
⅓ cup chopped roasted
    almonds
1 tablespoon (1 envelope)
    unflavored gelatine
heavy cream, unwhipped

Boil the rice in salted water for 5 minutes (plenty of water), drain, and put into a greased saucepan with the milk, orange peel, and butter. Cook over medium heat with the lid on until the rice is tender, about ½ hour. Take half the pineapple slices and cut them into pieces, combine with 2½ ounces cherries (keeping ½ ounce for garnish later), and soak in sherry and orange and lemon juice for 1 hour. When rice is cooked, combine it with the sugar, fruits, and juices, gently stir in the whipped cream, almonds, and the gelatine dissolved in some of the juice from the pineapple. Pour into individual molds, chill, and when quite set, turn out and decorate with the remaining pineapple slices cut in halves and some unwhipped cream and extra cherries on top. *Serves 6.*

RICE WITH PASSION FRUIT

When I was a small boy in Australia, my grandmother used to make this dish, which was simple because the passion fruit grew on a vine outside the house. Otherwise known as granadillas, passion fruit are being sold more and more around the world.

½ cup short-grain rice	*vanilla extract*
1¼ pints milk	*4 passion fruit*
3 ounces sugar	

Rinse the rice, put it in the milk, and add the sugar and a few drops of vanilla for flavor. Cook over medium heat for about 30 minutes, or until the rice is rich and creamy. Divide into 4 portions and serve in dessert dishes with the contents of 1 passion fruit scooped out on each bowl of rice (and extra sugar if required). *Serves 4.*

SOUTH AFRICAN BOBOTIE

Rice is not an integral part of African cookery, except in Arab areas or where Indian and Chinese descendants use their native recipes. But here is one from Cape Town.

2 tablespoons butter	*3 ounces seeded raisins*
2 onions, finely sliced	*2 eggs*
2 apples, peeled and diced	*1 teaspoon turmeric*
2 pounds ground meat (can be raw or cooked)	*salt and pepper*
	12 almonds, peeled
2 slices bread, soaked and squeezed	*6 lemon leaves (or bay leaves)*
2 tablespoons curry powder	*1¼ cups milk*
2 tablespoons sugar	*1 cup rice*
2 tablespoons vinegar	

Heat the butter in a pan, fry the onion and apple, then add the ground meat, bread, curry powder, sugar, vinegar, raisins, 1 egg, turmeric, and salt and pepper to taste. Stir well to beat the egg and get a good mixture. Chop the almonds into quarters and mix in. Place the mixture in a greased ovenproof dish. Stick the bay leaves upright in the mixture (or, if you can get lemon leaves, roll them up and push into the mixture) and bake in a moderate oven (350° F.) for about 30 minutes if the meat is cooked, or just over an hour if raw. Beat the remaining egg into the milk and pour this over the bobotie and cook for 10 minutes more.

While the bobotie is cooking, boil the rice to serve hot with it. Chutney and some fruits, as well as a salad of peppers, tomatoes, and onions, are also sometimes served with the dish. *Serves 6.*

RICE VERSATILITY

Rice in Soups

Rice made into soup? What's so surprising about that? Rice contains many nourishing elements, some of which would be boiled out into the water in the normal way of cooking rice, so why not add other flavorings and foods and get the benefit of the rice water in the soup? There are hundreds of ways of using rice in soup, and, indeed, many people in other countries keep the rice water for making soup even without using rice in the soup itself. Here are some of the more popular ways of preparing soups with rice in them.

AVGOLEMONO

This is one of the classic dishes of Greek cookery, although it is also well known in other parts of the Balkans.

5 pints strong chicken stock   *juice of 2 lemons*
½ cup rice   *salt and pepper*
4 eggs

In a good-sized saucepan bring the stock to a boil and add the rice. Bring to a boil again, reduce heat, and simmer for 25 minutes, or until rice is tender. Remove from the heat.

Beat the eggs until frothy, gradually work in the lemon juice; take about a cup of warm stock and rice and beat it into the egg and lemon, making sure that you beat it constantly until well mixed. Then add the egg-lemon mixture to the soup in the pan; reheat, but do not boil. Season with salt and pepper and serve immediately. *Serves 6.*

COCK-A-LEEKIE

Originally made by the Scots as a means of using a cock that had outlived its usefulness, cock-a-leekie, cock-a-leeky, or cocky-leeky was later extended to the hen past its prime. This is a really magnificent dish if properly prepared, since the old fowl has far more flavor for stewing than a younger one.

4 leeks	4 slices bacon
2 stalks celery	2 teaspoons salt
1 large carrot	pepper
1 large onion	1 bouquet garni
1 turnip	3 ounces rice
1 large old boiling fowl	
(cock if you really insist)	

Wash leeks and celery, scrape carrot, peel onion and turnip, roughly chop them all, and put them into a large saucepan or stewpot. Depending on the size of the fowl, place it whole or jointed in the pot on top of the vegetables. Lay bacon slices over top of fowl. Cover with water and add salt, pepper, and bouquet garni, bring to a boil, then reduce heat and simmer for at least 2 but preferably 3 or 4 hours. About 20 minutes or half an hour before serving, add rice and simmer until the rice is cooked. Avoid at all costs allowing the soup to boil, or the fowl will be tough.

The meat may be removed from the bird and served separately, or in the soup.   *Serves 4.*

CREAM OF RICE AND CARROT SOUP

¼ cup rice	1¼ pints stock
3 medium-sized carrots, sliced	cayenne pepper to taste
	salt to taste
1 stalk celery, sliced	⅓ cup cream
1 onion, chopped	finely chopped red pepper

Mix all ingredients, except cream and red pepper, and bring to a boil in a saucepan; lower heat and simmer for 25 minutes, or until vegetables and rice are tender. Put into an electric blender (or press through a sieve), then blend in cream. Put into the refrigerator, and when thoroughly chilled serve with a garnish of finely chopped red pepper. *Serves 4.*

CREAM OF RICE SOUP

4 tablespoons butter	6 ounces milk, boiled
⅓ cup rice flour	salt and pepper
2½ pints veal or chicken stock	1 egg yolk
	⅓ cup cream

Melt butter in a pan and make a roux with the rice flour. Stir in the stock, bring to a boil, and simmer gently for about 1 hour. Add milk, season to taste, and cook for a few minutes. Mix egg yolk and cream in the bottom of a tureen and stir in the hot soup.

This may now be used as the basis for a number of different soups that vary only in the flavoring added—see below. *Serves 5 to 6.*

CREAM OF RICE CLAMART SOUP

Ingredients: as for Cream of Rice Soup, plus 1½ pounds green peas.

Boil the peas with salt and a little sugar in the water, then drain them and make them into a purée, either in an electric blender or by pressing through a sieve. Gradually mix into the stock when adding the milk; otherwise follow the Cream of Rice Soup recipe. *Serves 4.*

LETTUCE CREAM OF RICE SOUP

½ cup rice
2½ pints Cream of Rice
  Soup (see above) but
  without egg and cream
1 head Boston lettuce (washed
  and torn into leaves)

salt and pepper
1 egg yolk
5 ounces cream
croutons of fried bread

Cook rice separately, drain, rinse, and keep hot.

Make Cream of Rice Soup up to the point of adding the egg yolk and cream. Blanch lettuce leaves, tear up, and put into the soup, boil, and then simmer for 1 hour. Press through a sieve or put through an electric blender, reheat, and season to taste. Complete the soup with the egg yolk and cream as for Cream of Rice Soup and serve with croutons of fried bread and the boiled rice. *Serves 4.*

Variations: Try Cream of Rice Soup with purée of carrots, asparagus, etc.

DUCK AND RICE SOUP

wings, neck, and giblets
  from 2 ducks
1 teaspoon salt
1 medium-sized onion,
  chopped
1 slice celeriac (celery
  root), chopped

1 cup long-grain rice
1 tablespoon butter
1 tablespoon flour
grated nutmeg

Put duck pieces and giblets into 2½ pints of water in a saucepan, add salt and the chopped onion and celeriac, bring to a boil, and simmer for 1½ hours. Strain liquid into another saucepan, bone the duck pieces, and chop meat and giblets into smallish pieces and set aside. Add rice to the strained liquid and cook about 20 minutes, or until rice is tender. Add duck meat and giblets to the soup, bring to a boil again, then thicken with a roux made with the butter and flour and season to taste with grated nutmeg. *Serves 4.*

INDIAN RICE SOUP

3 pints rice water
2 large onions, finely
chopped
hot red chilis, chopped, to
taste

ground white pepper, to taste
salt
juice of 1 lemon
2 tablespoons ground rice

An excellent way of using the water in which rice has been cooked. Put it into a saucepan, add the onions, chilis, and pepper, and bring to a boil. Reduce heat and simmer gently for 1 hour. Add salt and juice of the lemon, then thicken with the ground rice before serving. Since this is an Indian dish and for many may be an acquired taste, experiment first with the chilis and pepper before deciding on the amounts to be used. *Serves 4.*

MINESTRONE MILANESE

2 tablespoons butter
vegetable oil
1 onion, chopped
2 cloves garlic, crushed
4 ounces ham
1 cup kidney beans, cooked
1 cup peas
3 cups green cabbage
(shredded)
2 stalks celery, chopped
1½ cups spinach
(shredded)

3 carrots, washed and sliced
2 medium-sized tomatoes,
peeled and chopped
2 small potatoes, peeled
4 pints good clear stock
pinch of dried sage
3 sprigs of parsley
salt and pepper
½ cup rice
grated Parmesan cheese

Heat the butter and 1 tablespoon cooking oil in the bottom of a stock pot, add onion, and brown; add garlic, ham, cut into small strips, and all the vegetables, and cook over low heat for about 20 minutes. Now add the stock, sage, parsley, and seasoning, and simmer partially covered for 1 hour; add rice, adjust seasoning, and cook for another 30 minutes. Serve with grated Parmesan in a separate dish.   *Serves 6.*

MULLIGATAWNY SOUP

Mulligatawny might not be the popular soup it was in Victorian England, but if it is properly made and served, it is still a very good dish. Here is a classic recipe.

2 onions	*bouquet garni of bay leaves,*
2 carrots	*turmeric, coriander, and*
2 medium-sized greening	*grated lemon rind*
apples	*salt and pepper*
2 tablespoons shortening	*2 tablespoons shredded*
2 teaspoons strong curry	*coconut*
powder	*juice of 1 lemon*
1½ pounds lamb neck, cut	*2 tablespoons cornstarch,*
into cubes	*about*
	2 tablespoons rice

Peel and slice the onions, carrots, and apples; fry them in the shortening in a large saucepan until they are lightly browned. Add the curry powder and cook for a few minutes, then add the meat and 3¾ pints cold water. Drop the bouquet garni, tied in cheesecloth, into the pot, add seasoning to taste, bring to a boil, and then simmer gently with the lid on for 3 hours or more. After 1 hour add the shredded coconut, and just before serving, squeeze in the lemon juice and add enough cornstarch, mixed with water, to thicken the soup. Remove bouquet garni and serve, with rice, boiled separately, as accompaniment.   *Serves 4.*

PARTAN BREE, OR CRAB AND RICE SOUP

Goodness knows where the Scots got the name from, but the soup is a delightful one.

3 ounces rice	*1¼ pints chicken stock*
1¼ pints milk	*salt and pepper*
1 large crab (cooked, or the	*anchovy paste*
equivalent canned)	*⅓ cup cream*

Cook rice in milk, simmering for about 20 minutes, or until the rice is tender. Take meat from crab, setting aside the meat from the claws, which should be diced. Mash meat from body of the crab and add it to the milk and rice, then put mixture through an electric blender or press it through a sieve. Return to the saucepan, add stock, a small quantity at a time, and season to taste with salt, pepper, and anchovy paste. Simmer, without allowing it to boil, for about 15 minutes, then add remaining crab meat and the cream and stir until well heated, but not boiling.   *Serves 6.*

SHRIMP AND RICE SOUP

½ cup dry white wine	*good pinch thyme*
2 pints clear stock	*1 bay leaf*
¾ pound large fresh shrimp,	*1 tablespoon chopped*
shelled	*parsley*
3 tablespoons butter	*2 tablespoons chopped*
1 medium-sized onion,	*celery*
chopped	*¼ cup rice*
1 carrot, sliced	*salt and pepper*

Put the wine and about one quarter of the stock into a saucepan. Reserve 4 large shrimp for garnish and add the rest to pan; cook, covered, for 5 minutes over medium heat. Put 2 tablespoons butter into a pan and sauté the onion, carrot, thyme, bay leaf, parsley, and celery until golden. Strain shrimp liquid into this pan and add remaining stock. Bring to a boil, and meanwhile mash shrimp to a pulp and then return to the soup. Add rice and simmer until the rice is tender, about 20 minutes. Remove bay leaf and put the soup through a blender (or press through a sieve). Return to saucepan, add remaining butter, season to taste, and serve with large shrimp as garnish.   *Serves 4.*

RICE AND CHERVIL SOUP

2½ *pints white stock*
¼ *cup rice*
2 *tablespoons chopped*
　chervil
2 *tablespoons ground rice*

1¼ *cups milk*
pepper and salt
ground cinnamon
chopped chives

Put the stock in a saucepan, add rice and chopped chervil, bring to a boil, and simmer for 25 minutes; strain, add ground rice and milk, and simmer again for 15 minutes. Season with salt, pepper, and cinnamon to taste and garnish with chopped chives.   *Serves 4.*

RICE, LENTIL, AND LAMB SOUP

1 *pound boneless stewing*
　lamb
1 *tablespoon butter*
salt
freshly ground black pepper

½ *pound (about 1¼ cups)*
　lentils
1 *large onion, sliced*
1 *cup long-grain rice*

Cut the lamb into 1-inch squares and brown it in a pan with enough of the butter. Place lamb in a saucepan with 2 pints water, 1 teaspoon salt, and a good dash of black pepper. Bring to a boil, cover, and then simmer for 2½ hours. While this is cooking, wash the lentils, add them to the soup, and simmer for 15 minutes more. While soup is simmering, brown onions in the pan in which the lamb has been browned. Add these to the soup, washing out the pan with half a cup of soup and returning it to the saucepan. Add the rice and another 1¼ pints water and cover, then cook until all the ingredients are tender. This is a thick soup and, if necessary, the lid may be removed and the heat turned up when it is cooked to make it thicker. *Serves 4.*

RICE AND POTATO SOUP

1½ pounds potatoes (4 or 5 medium-sized), peeled and diced	salt and pepper
	3¼ pints clear stock
	1¼ pints milk
3 onions, sliced	2 ounces rice
1 stalk celery, chopped	

Put the diced potato in a saucepan with the onion, celery, salt and pepper, and the stock and cook over low heat until the vegetables are quite soft. Put through a sieve or blend in an electric blender, return to pot, and add the milk and rice; adjust seasoning. Simmer until rice is tender and serve in a tureen. *Serves 6.*

RICE AND PUMPKIN SOUP

2 ounces long-grain rice	salt and pepper
1½ pounds pumpkin	2 tablespoons butter
3 medium-sized potatoes	3 tablespoons heavy cream
3 large tomatoes	milk (optional)

Boil the rice in 2½ pints of salted water for about 15 minutes. Drain, and reserve water in which it was boiled. Rinse rice and set aside. Into the rice water put pumpkin, peeled and cut into smallish pieces, potatoes peeled and cut up, and tomatoes peeled and seeded. Season with salt and pepper and cook over low heat for ½ hour. Pass the soup through a sieve or purée in a blender, then add rice, butter, and cream (and a little milk if it is too thick) and reheat, but be careful not to boil it once the cream has been added.   *Serves 4.*

RICE AND TOMATO SOUP

2 ounces rice
1 16-ounce can tomatoes,
   or 1 pound fresh
1 carrot, sliced

1 large onion, chopped
1½ pints stock
6 celery seeds, tied in muslin
salt and pepper

Wash the rice well and place it and all the other ingredients except salt and pepper into a pan and bring to a boil. Season and simmer gently about ½ hour, until the rice and vegetables are tender. Remove bag of celery seeds and pass soup through a sieve, pressing the vegetables and rice through as well. Reheat, test for seasoning, and serve in a hot tureen.   *Serves 4.*

SHRIMP AND RICE SOUP

½ pound jumbo shrimp
2 cups fresh bread crumbs
1¼ pints fish stock
¼ cup cream

4 ounces rice
chopped parsley
1 hard-boiled egg yolk

Chop the shrimp very finely by hand or in a blender, mix with the bread crumbs and fish stock, and simmer for 1 hour. Return to the blender or press through a sieve; mix in cream and reheat without boiling. Meanwhile, boil, rinse, and dry the rice and keep it warm. Divide it among the plates and pour soup over, with garnish of chopped parsley and crumbled egg yolk. *Serves 4.*

Rice as an Appetizer

Rice lends itself in many ways to appetizer dishes because it combines so well with savory tastes like cheese, smoked fish, bacon, green and red peppers, shellfish, and so on. In addition to the recipes given in this section, there are very many more under the headings of various countries that can be used individually as appetizers.

RICE AND TOMATOES WITH OLIVES

8 ounces rice
wine vinegar
8 medium-sized tomatoes
freshly ground black pepper
mayonnaise

2 ounces button mushrooms,
*   canned or cooked fresh*
16 stuffed green olives
16 black olives, pitted
lemon juice

Cook the rice in plenty of boiling salted water for 18 minutes, drain, rinse in cold water, mix with a little wine vinegar, and cool in refrigerator. Halve the tomatoes crosswise and spoon out some of the seeds. Take one third of the rice, grind a little black pepper over it, and mix with just enough mayonnaise to bind it. Put a spoonful of this mixture into each tomato half. Chop the cooked mushrooms, mix into the remaining rice, and divide among 4 small dishes. Set the tomato halves 4 on each dish and top each rice-filled tomato half with 1 green and 1 black olive. Sprinkle the whole with a little lemon juice and serve cold. *Serves 4 to 8.*

EGG AND RICE AU GRATIN

6 ounces rice	salt and pepper
1¼ cups chicken stock (or 1 chicken cube in 1¼ cups water)	6 tablespoons butter
	grated Gruyère (or Cheddar) cheese
4 large eggs, soft-boiled, but not too runny	dried bread crumbs

Cook the rice in the chicken stock until tender, drain, and dry. Divide the rice among 4 small, greased ovenproof dishes or ramekins and smooth it so that it is flat. Cut the eggs lengthwise down the middle and place them yolk side down on the rice; season with salt and pepper. Melt the butter and pour over the eggs and rice, then sprinkle liberally with a mixture of grated cheese and a small amount of bread crumbs, and place under a hot broiler until nicely browned. *Serves 4.*

BACON, RICE, AND LETTUCE

6 ounces rice	pitted dates, chopped small
8 slices Canadian bacon, cooked crisp	salt and freshly ground black pepper
½ cup chopped walnuts	mayonnaise
2 hard-boiled eggs, chopped	lettuce
1 greening apple, peeled, cored, and chopped	1 beet, cooked and diced

Boil the rice in salted water for 20 minutes, then wash, drain, and dry. Make a mixture with the rice of the bacon, chopped small, walnuts, hard-boiled eggs, apple, and dates, season with salt and black pepper, add enough mayonnaise to bind together, and divide into 4 to 6 portions. Place each portion on either lettuce leaves or a bed of shredded lettuce on a small plate and garnish each with a small heap of diced beet on top. *Serves 4 to 6.*

SMOKED HADDOCK AND RICE

¾ pound smoked haddock fillet	*2 eggs and 2 egg yolks*
	grated Gruyère cheese
milk	*salt and pepper*
8 ounces rice, cooked	*dried bread crumbs*

Poach the haddock in water or milk until almost cooked, then shred into small pieces. Divide the rice into 4 parts and put 1 each in a ramekin or very small soufflé dish; divide the haddock into 4 and lay over the rice. Beat up the eggs and egg yolks with milk, add some cheese, season to taste, and pour into the ramekins. Sprinkle a little grated cheese and bread crumbs over, stand the ramekins in a baking dish with about an inch of water in it, and bake in a moderate oven (350° F.) about 40 minutes, or until the dish is firm and browned on top. *Serves 4.*

ARTICHOKES WITH RICE

4 artichokes	*8 ounces rice*
1 lemon	*1 pint stock*
5 slices Canadian bacon, diced	*2 medium-sized tomatoes, chopped and seeded*
2 tablespoons shortening	*bouquet garni*
1 large onion, chopped	*salt and pepper*

Trim the artichokes by taking off the bottom two rows of leaves and trimming the remainder with scissors. Then quarter them lengthwise and take away the chokes. Use a piece of lemon to rub them (in order to keep their color), blanch them in boiling water, and drain. Return to salted water and cook very gently for 45 minutes; drain and keep warm.

During this time fry the bacon gently in the shortening until half cooked. Remove the bacon and cook the onion until soft but not brown. Add the rice and cook until it is milky white and every grain covered in fat, add stock, and bring to a boil; add the remainder of the ingredients, except the artichokes, and simmer for 20 minutes, preferably in the oven at a moderate temperature (350° F.). When the rice is cooked and almost dry, remove the bouquet garni, mix in the artichoke quarters, and heat for 5 minutes in the oven before serving.   *Serves 4 to 6.*

ANDALUCIA TOMATOES

8 *medium-sized tomatoes*	12 *ounces rice, cooked*
1 *large onion*	2 *teaspoons Dijon mustard*
1 *green pepper*	*salt and pepper*
vegetable oil	8 *small radishes*
mayonnaise	*lettuce*

Slice the tops off the tomatoes and discard. Chop the onion and green pepper very finely, keeping a few strips of raw green pepper for garnish. Fry very lightly in oil the onion and chopped pepper, cool, then mix with mayonnaise, rice, Dijon mustard, and salt and pepper to taste, to make a filling. Scoop the centers out of the tomatoes and fill with the mixture, then garnish each with 1 radish and a few strips of green peppers. Serve on lettuce leaves.   *Serves 4 to 8.*

RICE AND VEGETABLE SALAD

12 ounces rice	2 medium-sized young carrots
1 red pepper	⅓ cup peas, frozen or fresh
1 green pepper	½ cup chopped green beans,
½ cucumber (or dill	frozen or fresh
cucumber)	oil and vinegar dressing
2 medium-sized tomatoes	salt and pepper

Boil the rice in salted water for 20 minutes, rinse well, drain, and cool. Blanch the peppers and cut into ½-inch squares, dice the cucumber and tomatoes, lightly boil the carrots, peas, and beans, and dice the carrots. Mix all ingredients together with cold rice, using only enough of the dressing to moisten the whole salad. This is generally prepared not more than about 1 hour before serving, during which time it should remain in the refrigerator. *Serves 4 to 6.*

Rice as an Accompaniment, Stuffing, or Garnish

Rice lends itself almost perfectly in many cases to the role of accompaniment to foods, either as an extra vegetable, or as a stuffing. In addition to the numerous recipes of this kind that appear in the various sections by country, here are a few more that will help vary your fare:

RICE AND FOIE GRAS STUFFING

8 ounces rice
1 pint strong chicken stock
1 3-ounce can truffled pâté
   de foie gras

1 onion, chopped
salt and pepper
1 egg, beaten

Cook the rice in the chicken stock in a tightly covered pan so that all the stock is absorbed. Mix the pâté, cut into small pats, with the rice and chopped onion, with salt and pepper to taste, and bind with the beaten egg. Quantities may be varied according to the size of the bird to be stuffed.

RICE, TANGERINE, AND CHESTNUT
   STUFFING

8 ounces rice
½ pound white bread,
   without crusts
5 ounces stock
4 tablespoons butter
2 large stalks celery, finely
   chopped

½ pound canned chestnut
   purée (or fresh chestnuts,
   boiled)
3 tangerines (or more,
   according to their size)
salt and pepper

This is suitable for very rich game, or goose, or perhaps very young duckling. Cook the rice in boiling salted water, drain, and cool. Soak the bread in the stock in a bowl, and when soaked, mash with a fork. Melt the butter and cook the celery for about 10 minutes, without browning. Now mix this with the mashed bread and stock, the chestnut purée (or mashed chestnut if cooked fresh), the cold rice, the sections of tangerine, seeded and halved, and salt and pepper to taste. Mix well with a wooden spoon or a fork.

GARNISHES

RICE À LA GRECQUE

4 tablespoons butter
8 ounces rice
1 pint stock
1 bouquet garni
2 ounces cooked meat
   (canned pork meat will
   do), diced

½ small red pepper,
   diced
⅓ cup green peas, frozen
   or fresh

Heat 2 tablespoons butter in a heavy pan, add the rice, and stir until thoroughly mixed. Add the stock and bouquet garni and bring to a boil, reduce heat, cover tightly, and simmer for 20 minutes. Remove bouquet garni. Add the diced meat, red pepper, and green peas and the remaining butter and leave in the oven or on very low heat only long enough to heat the meat and vegetables through. *Serves 4.*

RICE ESPAGNOLE

4 ounces bacon, chopped
1 onion, chopped
1 green pepper, chopped
1 red pepper, chopped
vegetable oil

1 clove garlic, crushed
8 ounces rice
1 pint stock
salt and pepper

Fry the bacon and onion and the green and red peppers in a little oil with the crushed garlic. After about 5 minutes add the rice, stir well to make sure it is properly mixed, add stock and seasonings, and simmer under tightly covered lid about 20 minutes, or until the mixture is slightly oily but not liquid.   *Serves 4.*

TOMATO RICE

1 onion, chopped
vegetable oil
4 ounces rice
1¼ cups stock

1 8-ounce can tomatoes
⅓ cup frozen peas
2 eggs, beaten
salt and pepper

Fry the onion in a little oil until brown, add the rice, and mix well. Add the stock, cover the pan, and simmer gently for about 15 minutes. Add the tomatoes, peas, and eggs, with salt and pepper to taste, re-cover, and cook for 5 minutes more, stirring once or twice.   *Serves 4.*

GREEN RICE

2 tablespoons vegetable
   oil
4 tablespoons finely chopped
   parsley
6 tablespoons scallions,
   green part only, chopped
1 medium-sized green pepper,
   chopped

3 tablespoons cooked spinach,
   chopped
8 ounces rice
1 pint stock
salt and pepper

Heat the oil and lightly fry the greens in a heavy pan. Add the rice and mix well, stir, then add the stock and seasoning. Cover with foil and a lid and put into a preheated moderate oven (350° F.) for 30 minutes, or until the rice is tender and the liquid absorbed. Mix in well to get the maximum green effect. *Serves 4.*

RICE WITH ORANGE

2 tablespoons chopped scallions, green part only	1 pint veal or chicken stock
4 stalks celery, chopped	2 oranges and the juice of 2 more
4 tablespoons butter	3 tablespoons raisins
8 ounces rice	salt and pepper

This is ideal for duckling, or roast pork, or other dishes with which orange flavor goes well.

Sauté the scallions and celery in the butter until tender, then add rice and stir in; cook until the rice begins to brown, and add stock and juice of all 4 oranges. Bring to a boil, grate in the peel of 2 oranges, add raisins and seasoning, cover tightly, and put into a preheated moderate oven (350° F.) for 40 minutes. *Serves 6.*

Rice for Dessert

Rice is almost perfect pudding material, particularly if you use the correct type of round-grain rice that would seem to be made for the purpose. But it is equally good in rice rings, or molds, or with fruit, and in a dozen other different ways.

ENGLISH RICE PUDDING

The traditional English rice pudding can be an extremely good dish if it is properly cooked and not dished up like the half-cooked horrors English children learn to detest at school. The commonest faults in cooking a rice pudding are: (1) insufficient milk to the amount of grain used and (2) baking the pudding too quickly. In each case the result is that the rice does not get the chance to absorb the liquid properly and so the pudding is not the creamy dish that it should be.

3 tablespoons short-grain rice	1¼ pints milk
	grated nutmeg
2 tablespoons sugar	

Wash the rice, drain, and put into a pie dish. Add the sugar and milk and stir. Some cooks let the rice soak in water for an hour, some like to let it soak in the milk for an hour before cooking. Sprinkle with grated nutmeg and put into a preheated slow oven (300° F.) for 2½ hours. *Serves 4.*

Rich Rice Pudding

Proceed as for English rice pudding (above), but add 2 beaten eggs to the mixture just before sprinkling with nutmeg and putting in the oven. *Serves 4.*

ENGLISH STEAMED RICE PUDDING

2 ounces short-grain rice	2 eggs, separated
1¼ pints milk	1 teaspoon grated lemon peel
2 tablespoons sugar	

Bring the rice to a boil in water, drain, add milk and sugar, and bring to a boil. Reduce heat and simmer until the rice is cooked, about 20 minutes. Cool. Mix in the egg yolks and lemon peel, beat up the egg whites until stiff, and fold into the mixture. Put it into a pudding basin or mixing bowl and steam over boiling water for about 40 minutes. *Serves 4.*

CARAMEL RICE

6 *tablespoons sugar (for caramel)*
1¼ *pints milk*
3 *tablespoons short-grain rice*

1 *tablespoon sugar (for rice)*
2 *eggs, beaten*
grated nutmeg

First make the caramel by dissolving the 6 tablespoons sugar in about 6 tablespoons of water and boiling until the syrup is a nice caramel color. Remove from heat. When it is cold, stir the milk into the syrup and heat very slowly on low heat until well blended. Wash the rice, drain, and place in a pie dish with a tablespoon of sugar, add the caramel milk, the beaten eggs, and a pinch of grated nutmeg, and bake in a preheated slow oven (300° F.) for 2½ hours. *Serves 4.*

TROPICAL FRUIT SALAD RICE SHAPE

4 *ounces short-grain rice*
1¼ *pints milk*
¾ *cup sugar*
1 *tablespoon (1 envelope) unflavored gelatine*
1 *tablespoon orange Curaçao*

1 *8-ounce can fruit salad*
1 *8-ounce can pineapple tidbits (or slices, cut up)*
5 *ounces cream, whipped*

Wash the rice, put it into the upper part of a double boiler with the milk, sugar, and gelatine, and cook until the rice is tender. Add the Curaçao, mix well, and turn out into a ring mold, or decorative mold if preferred. When set, turn out onto a serving dish and decorate with the fruits and whipped cream. If you used a ring mold, put the fruit salad in the center with an edging of whipped cream and the pineapple tidbits and their syrup around the base. *Serves 4.*

PEACH CONDÉ

4 ounces rice
1¼ pints milk
¼ cup sugar
1 16-ounce can peach
  halves, drained

1 cup red currant jelly
lemon juice

Cook the rice in the milk with the sugar over moderate heat for about 30 minutes or until thick and creamy (it should be stirred frequently). Divide the rice among 6 dessert dishes. Arrange peach halves on top of the rice and top with a little sauce made by heating the red currant jelly with a little water and a squeeze of lemon juice. *Serves 6.*

APPLE RICE TOFFEE

6 ounces rice
1 pound tart greening
  apples, peeled, cored, and
  sliced
¼ cup soft brown sugar
2 tablespoons lemon juice
1 teaspoon grated lemon peel

Toffee:
½ cup flour
1 teaspoon ground cinnamon
¾ cup soft brown sugar
½ cup butter or margarine

Mix together all the ingredients listed on the left, then put the mixture into a square ovenproof dish. Sift flour and cinnamon into another bowl, add sugar, then cut butter into this mixture until it is the size of small peas. Sprinkle this over the apple and rice mixture and put into a preheated moderate oven (350° F.) for 45 minutes. May be served hot or cold. *Serves 6 to 8.*

GROUND RICE PUDDING

¼ cup ground rice	*1¼ pints milk*
2 tablespoons vanilla sugar	*grated nutmeg*

Mix the ground rice and vanilla sugar in just enough cold milk to make a paste in a bowl. Put the remainder of the milk into a saucepan, bring to a boil, and pour over the rice and sugar. When mixed, pour back into the saucepan and add a pinch of grated nutmeg; simmer gently for 10 minutes.

Vanilla sugar is simply sugar in which a vanilla pod has been lying for a couple of weeks. If you have none, add a little vanilla extract with granulated sugar. *Serves 4.*

ORANGE RICE MOLD

12 ounces short-grain rice	*6 ounces heavy cream, whipped*
3¾ cups milk	
salt	*2 oranges, peeled and broken into sections*
juice of 2 oranges and grated peel of 1	
	2½ ounces Grand Marnier
3 ounces sugar	

Rinse the rice and drain, then put into a pan with the milk and a pinch of salt. Bring to a boil and simmer, covered, for about

30 minutes. Remove from heat and allow to stand for 15 minutes. Now mix in the orange juice, orange peel, sugar, and cream, put into a lightly buttered ring mold, and chill in the refrigerator for a few hours. While it is being chilled soak 2 oranges, peeled and broken into their sections, in the Grand Marnier. Turn out the ring mold and fill the center with the orange sections.   *Serves 6.*

RUM RICE FRITTERS

4 ounces short-grain rice	*½ cup flour*
1¼ pints milk	*2 tablespoons dark rum (or*
1 tablespoon butter	*more, according to taste)*
1 tablespoon sugar	*salt*
1 teaspoon lemon juice	*vegetable oil*
3 eggs, separated	*confectioners' sugar*

Boil the rice with the milk, butter, sugar, and lemon juice until the rice is mushy and almost dry. Allow it to cool. Add the egg yolks, flour, and rum and mix well. Allow the mixture to stand for a few hours before using. When ready to use, beat the egg whites, with a pinch of salt, until they are stiff, heat some oil in a pan until very hot, fold the egg whites into the rice mixture, and put a tablespoonful at a time into the very hot oil, frying until the fritters are a golden brown color. Drain, and sift confectioners' sugar over before serving.

The same mixture may be used for coating various fruits (already cooked) and deep-frying them.   *Serves 4.*

RICE AND FRUIT MERINGUE

4 ounces short-grain rice
1¼ pints milk
¼ cup sugar
2 large apples (or pears, etc.,
   or canned fruit), cooked
   in syrup

4 egg whites
1 cup superfine sugar
vanilla extract

Cook the rice as for Peach Condé (see page 162) and spread it over the bottom of a fairly shallow round ovenproof pie dish. Arrange cooked fruit on top of the rice with only enough of the fruit syrup so that the finished dish will not be too sloppy. Make a meringue mixture by beating the egg whites and, when soft peaks form, beating in the sugar gradually, a tablespoonful at a time, and adding a few drops of vanilla. Cover fruit with mixture, decorating with some of the mixture through a pastry bag if desired. Dredge lightly with sugar and bake in a preheated slow oven (300° F.) until cooked. *Serves 4.*

RASPBERRY RICE

3 ounces short-grain rice
1¼ pints milk
2 tablespoons sugar
grated nutmeg

1 package (for 1 pint)
   raspberry gelatin dessert
orange slices for garnish

Soak the rice 1 hour in cold water, drain, add the milk, and simmer until the mixture is creamy and the rice *al dente.* Mix in the sugar and a good pinch of grated nutmeg. Dissolve the gelatin in about 1 pint boiling water and allow to cool. Put a mold in the refrigerator or freezer until it is quite cold, then pour a little of the gelatin solution into it to form a coating on the inside of the cold mold. Mix the remaining gelatin with the rice, and as it is about to set, pour it into the mold and place in the refrigerator (or in a cool place). When quite set, dip the mold into hot water and turn out the dessert. Top with slices of fresh orange. *Serves 6.*

PINEAPPLE RICE FRITTERS FLAMBÉ

4 ounces short-grain rice	Fritter batter:
1¼ cups milk	*2 eggs, separated*
superfine sugar	*1 tablespoon melted butter*
2 tablespoons kirsch	*⅓ cup milk*
vegetable oil	*4 tablespoons flour*
8 slices canned pineapple	*pinch of salt*
2 tablespoons brandy	

Put the rice into the milk, with about 2 teaspoons of sugar, and bring to a boil, reduce heat, and simmer until the rice is cooked but still soggy enough to form into 8 flat rounds slightly larger than a slice of the pineapple. Before forming rice into the rounds, flavor it with half the kirsch. Beat egg whites until stiff peaks form. Beat the egg yolks, butter, and milk together, sift in the flour and salt, and fold in the egg whites. Dip the rounds in the fritter batter and cook in very hot oil until golden brown and crisp. Set aside and keep warm.

Meanwhile, marinate the pineapple slices in the rest of the kirsch. Put the rice fritters in a chafing dish, each topped with a slice of pineapple; moisten with a little pineapple juice, sprinkle well with superfine sugar. Heat the chafing dish over a spirit lamp. Heat the brandy in a ladle, set it alight, and pour it over the pineapple rings on their fritters. Serve quickly before the flame dies out, if possible. It may be necessary to cook these in two lots. *Serves 4.*

Rice with Cakes and Pastry

When rice is going through the milling process to which it is subjected before being sold, some of it is ground into flour of varying degrees of fineness and used in the making of various forms of cakes, pastry, and the like. The coarsest form is ground rice, which is available as Cream of Rice cereal.

Rice flour, which is almost as fine as ordinary flour, is better in shortbreads, some cookies, such as macaroons, and some cakes. It is also used in some desserts and puddings as well, and in confectionery.

RICE CAKE

This is made in a similar way to an ordinary cake, but half the flour is replaced by rice flour (or the whole of the flour may equally be replaced) and thus it achieves a slightly lighter result.

¾ cup butter or margarine
¾ cup superfine sugar
1½ cups unsifted flour
1 cup unsifted rice flour

1½ teaspoons baking powder
2 eggs, beaten
confectioners' sugar

Cream the butter and add the superfine sugar. Beat well. Sift the flour, rice flour, and baking powder into a mixing bowl, then stir in the butter and sugar mixture, then the eggs, mixing well. Put into a baking tin lined with greased baking parchment and bake in a preheated moderate oven (350° F.) for 1½ hours. Test with skewer and continue baking, if necessary, until cake is cooked through. Cool on wire rack and dredge with a little confectioners' sugar.

FRUIT CAKE WITH GROUND RICE

¾ *cup butter or margarine*
½ *cup sugar*
2 eggs
½ *cup plus 1 tablespoon*
  ground rice
1 cup unsifted flour

1 teaspoon cream of tartar
½ *teaspoon bicarbonate of*
  soda
¾ *cup raisins*
milk (*optional*)

Cream the butter and sugar, add each egg separately, and beat in well. Gradually mix in the ground rice, flour, cream of tartar, and bicarbonate of soda, and then the raisins. If necessary, use a little milk to make the mixture more workable.

Turn into a cake tin lined with greased paper and put into a preheated moderately hot oven (375° F.) and bake until cooked, about 1 hour.

PLAIN CAKE WITH GROUND RICE

½ *cup sugar*
½ *cup butter*
2 eggs
¾ *cup unsifted flour*

3 ounces ground rice
1 teaspoon baking powder
milk (*optional*)

Cream the sugar and butter; beat eggs until frothy, add to the creamed sugar and butter. Sift the flour, ground rice, and baking powder into the bowl with the creamed sugar and butter and eggs; mix lightly. If the mixture is too thick, add a little milk. Turn into a cake tin lined with greased paper and bake in a preheated moderately hot oven (375° F.) for about 45 minutes.

RICE CUPCAKES

¼ *cup superfine sugar*	¼ *teaspoon baking powder*
4 *tablespoons butter*	*vanilla extract*
1 *egg yolk*	*confectioners' sugar*
½ *cup flour*	8 *candied cherries*
¼ *cup ground rice*	

Cream the sugar and butter, then beat the egg yolk and mix in. Gradually add the flour, rice, and baking powder, sifted together, to the mixture, stirring in well. Add a few drops of vanilla for flavoring, mix well again, and let stand for 30 minutes. Divide the mixture among 8 muffin cups, or separately on a greased baking sheet, and bake in a preheated hot oven (450° F.) until cooked (about 10 minutes). Cool on a wire tray, top with a little vanilla-flavored icing and a candied cherry each. (For icing, beat confectioners' sugar with a little water, adding a few drops vanilla, until glossy.)

RICE CAKES

¾ *cup sugar*	1 *teaspoon baking powder*
¾ *cup butter or margarine*	¾ *cup currants*
3 *eggs*	3 *ounces candied peel*
½ *cup plus 1 tablespoon*	*flavoring extract*
ground rice	*milk (optional)*
1½ *cups unsifted flour*	

Cream sugar and fat; beat eggs one by one into the creamed mixture. Sift rice, flour, and baking powder together. Pick over the currants, chop the peel, and add these to rice-flour mixture. Mix into the creamed mixture, add a little flavoring extract (vanilla, lemon, etc.), mix well, adding a little milk if mixture is too thick, and put into greased muffin cups. Bake in a preheated hot oven (450° F.) for a few minutes, then reduce temperature slightly and bake for another 15 minutes, or until cooked.

RICE-DATE LOAF

1⅓ cups rice flour	1 egg
1 teaspoon baking powder	¼ cup milk
salt	¼ cup dates, pitted and
2 tablespoons butter	chopped

Sift the rice flour, baking powder, and a pinch of salt into a mixing bowl. Melt the butter and add it to the flour; beat the egg into the milk and add it and the chopped dates to the mixture, and stir well. When quite mixed turn into a cake tin and bake in a preheated moderate oven (350° F.) for 45 minutes. Cool on a wire rack before turning out of the tin.

GROUND RICE AND LEMON CAKE

6 tablespoons butter	3 eggs, separated
¾ cup superfine sugar	¾ cup plus 2 tablespoons
grated peel of ½ lemon	ground rice

Cream the butter and sugar and beat in the lemon peel. Beat in the egg yolks one at a time; stir in the ground rice; beat the egg whites until they are stiff enough to form peaks, then fold them into the cake mixture. Bake in a preheated moderate oven (350° F.) for about 1 hour or until cooked.

MACAROONS

These are not only very tasty by themselves, but may be used as the basis for a number of dessert dishes.

rice paper	*3 egg whites*
⅓ cup rice flour	*flavoring extract*
1½ cups ground almonds	*1½ ounces blanched whole*
1½ cups superfine sugar	*almonds*

Cut the rice paper into squares according to size desired; heat oven to moderate (350° F.). Mix the rice flour, ground almonds, and sugar in a bowl, lightly beat the egg whites and beat into the rice and sugar mixture for 5 minutes, then add a few drops of flavoring extract (vanilla, almond, etc., as preferred) and beat for 5 minutes more. Spoon out (or pass through a pastry bag) onto the pieces of rice paper and put into the oven with 1 or 2 almonds on top of each macaroon. Bake for 20 minutes, remove, cool on a wire rack, and trim off excess rice paper.

RICE AND COCONUT MACAROONS

1½ cups shredded coconut	*whites of 3 eggs*
3 tablespoons rice flour	*rice paper*
¼ cup superfine sugar	

Mix the coconut, rice flour, and sugar well together. Beat the egg whites until quite stiff, then fold in carefully with the coconut mixture. Spoon out onto pieces of rice paper and bake for 25 minutes in a preheated moderate oven (350° F.).

Rice for Health

Since this is a book about rice, let's take a look at the effect of this foodstuff on the health of man. Before going into the question too deeply, however, it should be remarked that anything that has been the staple diet of half the world's population for as long as rice cannot be all that bad. Recently I read an article in an American magazine by a well-known British record producer, Ray Horricks, and he has graciously allowed me to quote some of it:

Actually becoming macrobiotic is rather like joining the Vietcong without having to go into the jungle and fight Americans. Ten days of nothing but short-grain brown rice and boiled water. Put off already? Don't be; it gets easier and pleasanter after this, while there are mental and physical compensations. Keith Michell first introduced me to it. I was producing his LP *Keith Michell Sings Ancient and Modern*. At the same time he was appearing in a West End play and preparing for a TV spectacular—and looking ridiculously healthy and energetic. Backstage his pies made with wholemeal flour and vegetables tasted delicious. So did his brown rice cooked with onion, parsley and a few prawns added. I even liked the milder flavor of the dandelion coffee he brought to the recording sessions.

Keith said I was "sanpaku." That is, I had an area of white showing between the iris of my eye and the lower lid. It denoted being out of condition and the degree of anguish that accompanies this. After years of drinking gin-and-tonics and eating plastic chicken and the tissue-paper we call English bread it was hardly surprising! Anyway I decided to make the change. And even before the ten-day cleansing period was over, when I moved on to the wider macrobiotic diet, life had become an enjoyable experience again.

Whether you want to go on a macrobiotic diet or not, it shows at least that you can live on brown rice and boiled water for ten days, and feel better for it. Recently I was forced to go on a very strict diet, some 1,000 calories a day, and in such diets just about everything except boiled eggs, small quantities of lean meat, some salad, and some fruit is banned. The diet did allow three thin slices of bread a day, and the dietitian, a rather evasive lady, finally did admit that I could have six ounces of rice a day instead of the bread. And much more enjoyable it was too, particularly since I would not have been allowed butter with the bread. But that was a very tough diet, and in most other diets rice is on the happier side of things because it has fewer calories and comes out very favorably in a comparative carbohydrate count, as you can see from the following:

	GRAMS OF CARBOHYDRATE PER OUNCE	CALORIES PER OUNCE
Rice (cooked)	8½	35
Potatoes (boiled)	5½	23
Potatoes (french-fried)	10½	68
Crispbreads	22	98
White bread (ordinary)	15	75
Spaghetti and macaroni	7	32

From the above you will see that pasta and boiled potatoes are lower on the list than rice. But boiled potatoes are not very tasty unless they have been covered in butter, or mashed, or in some way treated with another food that will push the carbohydrate and calorie values way up. Rice can be eaten without such treatment. Spaghetti and macaroni also need some accompaniment to make them tasty.

Apart from the main causes of obesity, such as calories, carbohydrates, and so on, there are other considerations of diet for modern man, such as keeping down the cholesterol level in the blood in the case of heart and circulation complaints. This requires a low-fat diet, and in such diets, rice can play an important part because, once the outer husks have been milled from rice (which is how stores normally supply it), its fat content is down to something like 0.2 milligrams per ounce weight of cooked rice. Because of this, and because it is so versatile, rice can be combined with many low-fat foods to produce dishes that are within the prescribed fat level but are still attractive enough to keep the patient within his diet. One of the great troubles with dieting is that if the regime becomes too overpowering or monotonous, the patient is likely to start going over the limit.

Although the protein value of rice is low, it is still twice as great as that of the potato, and the amino-acid structure of rice is such that it is more beneficial to man than most other food grains. The fact that rice is usually digested within one-half to one-quarter of the time it takes to digest other foods must mean fewer aftereffects to many people and will certainly be good for anyone who suffers from digestive trouble. It is also said to be a far more bland food than others, greatly advantageous to those with intestinal disorders. Those who are allergic to some foods can usually take rice without any fear of coming out in a rash, and its low sodium content makes it a permissible item in diets that must remain salt-free to counter high blood pressure and some heart and kidney diseases.

For those who, for whatever reason, count their calories, here are a few recipes for which the British Rice Council has worked out an exact calorie count based on ratings for American long-grain rice. These recipes are not, of course, for people on very strict diets, but they will certainly be a help for those who want to control their daily intake of calories.

BAKED PORK STEAKS AND RICE

2 tablespoons margarine
1½ pounds pork
    fillet, cut into 6
1½ teaspoons salt
¼ teaspoon pepper

¾ cup rice
2 pints boiling chicken stock,
    fat skimmed off
1 medium-sized onion,
    chopped

Heat the margarine in a pan and brown the pork fillets. Remove from pan, and season with salt and pepper. Add rice to the pan and cook, stirring constantly, until it is browned. Add stock and onion and put into a large casserole; stand pork on top and cover. Put into a moderate oven (350° F.) and bake for 40 minutes. *453 calories each for 6 persons.*

MEXICANA CHICKEN AND RICE

2 tablespoons margarine
¾ cup rice
1 tomato
1 clove garlic, crushed
1 large onion, chopped

1 2½-pound roasting
   chicken, jointed
1 teaspoon salt
½ teaspoon chili powder
¼ teaspoon pepper

Heat 1 tablespoon margarine over moderate heat and brown the rice; peel and chop tomato and add it and garlic and onion to the rice, stirring again and cooking for a few minutes more. Heat remaining margarine in a heavy saucepan and brown the chicken joints in it. When the chicken is almost cooked, add the rice mixture, seasonings, and 1 pint water. Bring to a boil, stir once, cover tightly, and simmer gently for 15 minutes or until chicken and rice are tender. *296 calories each for 6 persons.*

LOUISIANA TUNA AND RICE

¾ cup rice
1 onion, sliced
2 tablespoons butter or
   margarine
2 tablespoons flour

1 16-ounce can tomatoes
chopped parsley
salt and pepper
1 7-ounce can tuna

Put rice into a pan with 1 pint water and some salt, bring to a boil, stir, cover, reduce heat, and simmer for 15 minutes. Fry onion in butter until golden, then add flour and blend, add tomatoes, parsley, and seasonings, and stir until thickened. Flake the tuna and stir it into the mixture; when heated through, spoon the mixture over the rice and serve.   348 *calories each for 4 persons.*

HEARTY RICE MEAL

2 tablespoons margarine
1 pound ground beef
4 medium-sized carrots,
   sliced
1½ cups frozen or canned
   green peas

1 clove garlic, crushed
salt and pepper
generous ½ cup rice
1 tablespoon flour

Heat the margarine and fry beef until browned; drain off excess fat. Add carrots, peas, garlic, 1 pint water, and seasoning and simmer for 5 minutes. Stir the rice into the mixture, bring to a boil, and stir once, then cover tightly and simmer for 15 minutes or until rice and vegetables are tender. Blend flour smoothly with another ¼ pint water and stir into the rice. Cook for 5 minutes more, then serve.   210 *calories each for 8 persons.*

BEEF AND RICE CASSEROLE

¾ cup rice
1 package onion soup mix
1 tablespoon butter or
   margarine

12 ounces corned beef,
   chopped

Spread the rice in a shallow baking tin and put into a preheated moderately hot oven (400° F.), stirring occasionally, until the rice is toasted to a golden brown. Now put the rice, soup mix, butter, and beef in a baking dish with 1 pint boiling water. Stir well, cover with foil or lid, and bake at 350° F. for 40 minutes. *275 calories each for 6 persons.*

GREEN AND GOLD RELISH

3 ounces rice, boiled and cooled

2 8-ounce cans crushed pineapple, drained

¾ cup grated raw carrot

4 medium-sized celery stalks, diced

2 tablespoons lemon juice

2 teaspoons grated lemon peel

¼ cup sugar

Combine all the ingredients and mix well. Cover and put in the refrigerator for 2 hours. Use as a salad or accompaniment for meat. *75 calories each for 8 persons.*

LEMON RICE FLUFF

1 package lemon pie filling mix

2 eggs, separated

½ cup superfine sugar

½ cup rice, cooked and kept warm

8 tablespoons shredded coconut, toasted

Mix the lemon pie mix, egg yolks, half the sugar, and 1¼ pints water. Cook, stirring continuously, until the mixture is thick. Fold in cooked rice and cool slightly; beat egg whites until stiff, then add remaining sugar and beat until very stiff. Fold in lemon pie filling. Chill thoroughly and serve in glasses with the coconut sprinkled on top. *202 calories each for 8 persons.*

Rice for the Freezer

You could boil rice and put it in the freezer until you need it, but it would hardly be worth while wasting that much space in your freezer. The time taken in defrosting and reheating the rice would be as long as or longer than it takes to boil some fresh rice from the box. Or, for that matter, you can buy instant rice, rice that has been precooked and then dehydrated: there would hardly be any difference in flavor. In any case, boiled rice will keep quite well in the refrigerator for a couple of weeks if it is covered to prevent it from drying out.

There are many ways that some of the recipes in this book may be prepared and then frozen, but the cook will need to consult a book on freezing to see what should and what should not be put into the freezer. For a start, do not put curry there: the chances of its contaminating other foods are too great to be worth the risk. If you are freezing any of the soups, when packing, remember to leave space at the top for expansion; remember also that those with cream added just before serving should be frozen without the cream, which can be added when reheating. Likewise, any soup containing garlic should be made without the garlic and have it added when reheating. Some accompaniments containing rice, for instance Rice with Orange to go with duckling, should be quite successful when thawed out after not too long in the freezer. Most of the desserts, particularly those with fresh fruit, will freeze well, but here again, remember that whipped cream, lemon juice, and other such last-minute additions should be left until the dish is defrosted and being served.

Rice flour is used in some dishes for the freezer, and if an equivalent amount of rice flour is substituted for some of the flour used in the pastry, the keeping properties of the pastry will be improved.

Index